MEDITATIONS ON A THEME

Meditations on a Theme

A spiritual journey

by

Metropolitan Anthony of Sourozh M.D. D.D.

MOWBRAYS
LONDON & OXFORD

© *Metropolitan Anthony* 1971

Printed in Great Britain by
Lowe & Brydone Printers Limited, Thetford, Norfolk

ISBN 0 264 64571 5

First Published in 1972

Sixth impression 1976

CONTENTS

ACKNOWLEDGEMENTS

The thanks of the author and publishers are due to SPCK for their permission to quote an extract from *The Way of the Pilgrim*.

M.T.A.

PREPARATION FOR THE JOURNEY

Girding our Loins

CONTRARY to what many think or feel a period of spiritual endeavour (during Lent, perhaps, or while taking part in a retreat) is a time of joy because it is a time for coming home, a period when we can come back to life. It should be a time when we shake off all that is worn and dead in us in order to become able to live, and to live with all the vastness, all the depth and all the intensity to which we are called. Unless we understand this quality of joy, we shall make of it a monstrous, blasphemous caricature, when in God's very name we make our life a misery for ourselves and for those who must pay the cost for our abortive attempts at holiness. This notion of joy coupled with strenuous effort, with ascetical endeavour, with struggle indeed, may seem strange, and yet it runs through the whole of our spiritual life, the life of the Church and the life of the Gospel, because the Kingdom of God is to be *conquered*. It is not something which is simply given to those who leisurely, lazily wait for it to come. For those who would wait for it in that spirit, it will come indeed: it will come at the dead of night, it will come like the Judgement of God, like the thief who takes us unawares, like the bridegroom who comes when the foolish virgins are asleep. This is not the way in which we should await the Kingdom and the Judgement. We must recapture an attitude of mind which, usually, we cannot conjure even out of our depth, something which has become strangely alien to us—the joyful expectation of the Day of the Lord—in spite of the fact that we know that this day will be a day of Judgement. It is striking to hear in church that we are proclaiming the Gospel, the gladdening news, of Judgement, but we are proclaiming that the Day of the Lord is not fear but hope and, together with the Holy Spirit, the Church can say: 'Come, Lord Jesus, come quickly!' As long as we are incapable of speaking in those terms we are missing something very important in our Christian consciousness. We are still, whatever we may say, pagans dressed up in evangelic garments. We are still people for whom God is a God outside, for whom his coming is darkness and dread, whose judgement is not our redemption but our condemnation, for whom a meeting face to face is a fearful event and not the hour we long and live for.

Unless we realise this, spiritual endeavour cannot be a joy, for it is strenuous and confronts us with judgement and responsibility—because we must judge ourselves in order to change and become able to meet the Day of the Lord, the glorious Resurrection, with an open heart, without hiding our face, ready to rejoice that he has come. And every coming of the Lord is judgement. The Fathers of the Church draw a parallel between Christ and Noah and they say that the presence of Noah among his generation was at the same time condemnation and salvation. It was condemnation because the presence of *one* man who had remained faithful, just one man, who could be a saint of God, was evidence that that was possible, and that those who were sinners, those who had rejected God and turned away from him, could have done likewise. So the presence of the righteous one was judgement and condemnation upon his time. Yet it was also the salvation of his time, because he was the only one thanks to whom God looked with mercy upon man. And the same is true of the coming of Christ.

There is another joy in judgement. It is not something which descends upon us from outside. The day will come when we shall stand before God and be judged, but as long as our pilgrimage continues, as long as we live in the process of becoming, as long as there is ahead of us this road that leads to the full measure of the stature of Christ which is our vocation, judgement must be pronounced by ourselves. There is a continuing dialogue within us throughout our life. You remember the parable in which Christ says: 'Make your peace with the adversary as long as you are in the way', and some of the spiritual writers have seen in the adversary not the devil indeed—with whom we cannot make our peace, with whom we are not to come to terms—but our conscience, which throughout life walks apace with us, which at no moment leaves us in peace. It is in continuous dialogue with us, gainsaying us at every moment, and we must come to terms with it, otherwise a moment will come when we shall come before the Judge and then this adversary

will be an accuser against us and we shall stand condemned. So that, on the road, judgement is something
which is happening all the time within us; there is a
dialogue, a dialectical tension between our thoughts,
emotions, feelings, actions and our conscience, which
stands in judgement upon us and before which we
stand in judgement.

But in this respect we very often walk in darkness,
and this darkness is the result of our darkened mind, of
our darkened heart, of our darkened eye, and it is only
if the Lord Himself sheds his light into our soul, upon
our life, that we can begin to see what is wrong and
what is right in it. There is a remarkable passage in the
writings of Father John of Kronstadt, a Russian priest
of the turn of the nineteenth century, in which he says
that God does not reveal to us the ugliness of our souls
unless he can espy in us sufficient faith and sufficient
hope for us not to be broken by the vision of our own
sins. In other words, whenever we see ourselves with
our dark side, as this knowledge increases, as we can
understand ourselves more in the light of God, that is,
in the light of the Divine Judgement, it means two
things: it means, indeed, that we sadly discover our
own ugliness, but also that we can rejoice at the same
time, because God has granted us his trust. He has
entrusted to us a new knowledge of ourselves as we
are, as he always saw us and as, at times, he did not
allow us to see ourselves because we could not bear the
sight of truth. And here again judgement becomes joy,
because although we discover what is wrong, yet this
discovery is conditioned by the knowledge that God

has seen enough faith, enough hope and enough fortitude in us to allow us to *see*, because he knows that now we can *act*. All that is important if we want to understand that joy and spiritual endeavour go together. Otherwise the continued, the insistent, effort of the Church, of the Word of God, to make us aware of what is wrong in us can lead to despair and darkening of the mind and soul. Then when we have become too depressed and low in spirit, we are incapable of meeting the Resurrection of Christ with joy, because then we realise, or imagine we realise, that this has nothing to do with us. We are in darkness, he is light. Nothing appears to us but our judgement and our condemnation, at the very moment when we should emerge out of darkness into the saving act of God which is both our judgement and our salvation.

And so the first step is to get to know ourselves. Sin is dividedness, both within ourselves and with regard to others, and among these others we must not forget our invisible Neighbour, God. The first step therefore in our evaluation of ourself will be to measure this state of disruption. How much are my heart and my mind at variance with one another? Is my will directed to one unique goal, or is it incessantly wavering? How far are my actions directed by my convictions, how far are they under the sway of unruly impulses? Is there any wholeness within me? On the other hand, how separated am I from God and my neighbour? This opposition between oneself and one's neighbour begins at the moment when we assert ourselves because, in doing so, we always distance ourselves from the other

5

and reject him. It is not in vain that Sartre has said 'Hell is other people'. But while we exclude the other we imprison ourselves also in irremediable loneliness so that in the end the same French writer could say 'Hell is ourselves'. This assertion of self is a sign of insecurity and lack of fulfilment. Also a measure of our lack of love, because love is forgetful of self and affirms the loved ones. It reveals an uncertainty with regard to the vigour of our being and our inability to trust other people's love. We assert ourselves to be sure that our existence is recognised and that our own being is not endangered, and by so doing we become small and void of content.

Yet when we try to appraise love itself or, rather, that amount of love which is within us, we may make many a sad discovery. How many people do we love? Two, three, hardly more, if loving means being more concerned for them than for myself. But what does our love mean to them? Is our love always a joy to them? Does our love set them free, does it give them an impulse to love and to rejoice? Does it not happen all too often that if the victims of our love dared to speak they would plead: 'Oh, please love me less but leave me free, I'm a prisoner of your love; because you love me you want to determine all my life, you want to shape all my happiness. If only you did not love me, I could be myself!' Does that not happen all too often between parents and children, friends, and husbands and wives? How costly our love is to others and how cheap it is for us, and yet Christ's command is that we should love one another as he loves us; to give his life

6

was his way of loving: we could begin with much less than giving our lives, but we should begin with the commandment Christ gives to the selfish, the most selfish of us—'Do unto others what you wish them to do to you'. You want to be happy; do so, but with justice. Give to your neighbour exactly as much as you claim for yourself. You want happiness—give an equal measure of happiness; you want freedom—give freedom in exactly the same measure. You want food, give food; you want love, unselfish and thoughtful—give unselfish and thoughtful love.

And then let us beware of what St John Chrysostom called 'the dark side of devilish love'. More often than not to love a person means to reject other people, either because our hearts are too narrow or because we feel duty bound for the sake of loyalty to the ones, to hate those whom they call their enemies, but this is not Christian love—not even human love. I remember how impressed I was at the moment of the invasion of Czechoslovakia, when I met Dr Hromadka, one of the leaders of the Church in that country. I had known him for many years and when we met he said to me: 'Tell everyone not to hate our invaders for love of us; those who hate the ones for the sake of the others give a free hand to the devil.' He was engaged and committed to the fight, yet he knew where the real battle took place, in the hearts of men, between love and hatred, light and darkness, God and him who is the murderer from the beginning. To choose the ones in order to love them, to reject the others in order to hate them, whichever side you take, only adds to the sum total of hatred and darkness. And the devil finds his own profit in it; he does not mind whom you hate; once you hate, you have opened a door for him to walk through, to creep into your heart, to invade a human situation. The love which Christ teaches us is incompatible with hatred of the other, we must learn to 'discern the spirit of God from the spirit of the prince of this world', and the touchstone is humility and selfless love. And love includes myself also.

We must learn not only to accept our neighbour, but also to accept ourselves; we tend too easily to consider that all that we like in ourselves is our true self, while all that we and others find ugly is only accidental. I am the real, attractive self, circumstances are distorting my best intentions, queering the pitch for my most perfect impulses. We might usefully remember a page from the correspondence of one of the Russian staretz, Macarius of Optina, taken from an exchange of letters he had with a merchant of St Petersburg: 'My maid has left me and my friends recommend a village girl to replace her—what do you advise me to do? Shall I hire her or not?' 'Yes', answered the staretz. After a while his correspondent writes again. 'Father, allow me to dismiss her, she is a real demon, since she has come I spend my time in rage and fury and have lost all control over myself!' And the staretz replies: 'Take care not to dismiss her, she is an angel whom God has sent to you to make you see how much anger was hidden within you, which the previous maid had never been able to reveal to you.' So it is not circumstances that make shadows darken our souls, nor is it God's fault, although we accuse him all the time. How often have I heard people say 'Here are my sins', then stop a moment to take a breath and begin a long discourse to the effect that had not God afflicted them with such a hard life, they would not sin so much. 'Of course', they would say, 'I am in the wrong, but what can I do with such a son-in-law, my rheumatism or the Russian revolution?' And more than once I suggested, before reading a prayer of absolution, that peace between God and man was a two-way traffic, and I asked whether the penitent was prepared to forgive God all his misdeeds, all the wrong he had done, all the circumstances which prevented this good Christian from being a saint. People do not like this, and yet, unless we take full responsibility for the way we face our heredity, our situation, our God and ourselves, we shall never be able to face more than a small section of our life and self. If we want to pass a true and balanced judgement on ourselves we must consider ourselves as a whole, in our entirety.

Certain things in us belong already, however incipiently, to the Kingdom of God. Others are still a chaos, a desert, a wilderness. And it is for us by hard toil and inspired faith to make them into the Garden of Eden; as Nietzsche says, 'One must possess a chaos within to give birth to a star.' And we must have faith in the chaos, pregnant with beauty and harmony. We must look at ourselves as an artist looks, with vision and sobriety, at the raw material which God has put into his hands and out or which he will make a work of art, an integral part of the harmony, the beauty, the truth and the life of the Kingdom. A work of art is determined both by the artist's vision and the character of the material he is given. We cannot use any material to any purpose indiscriminately; an ivory crucifix cannot be made out of granite, nor a Celtic cross out of Greek marble. An artist must learn to discern the peculiar potentialities of the given material and call out of it all the beauty hidden in its depth. So must every one of us discern in himself under God's guidance and with the help of his wiser friends, his particular capabilities and characteristics, both good and bad, and make use of them to achieve in the end that work of art which is his true self. To use a phrase of St Irenaeus of Lyon, 'the splendour of God is a man fully realised'.

The way to achieve this may be a winding way and there are moments when, to build the good, we may have to lean on what is later to be eradicated. We find in the life of Mahatma Gandhi a very enlightening story. At the end of his career he was accused of having been inconsistent in his preaching. It was said that in the early days he had called out the dockers on strike and it was only after the battle was won that he began to advocate non-resistance. He gave a very wise answer. 'These men', he said, 'were cowards, I taught them violence to overcome their cowardice and then non-resistance to subdue their bellicosity.' Was not his realism wiser and more effective than preaching meekness or humility to men who would label with these holy names their cowardice? Was it not a truer way for their spiritual growth to give them inducements such as they would understand and make sure that their progress was real at every step? We also may need over longer or shorter periods of time the drive which our less noble impulses afford us, provided we later outgrow our immaturity. Martin Buber in the *Tales of the Hasidim* related the story of a man who asked a Rabbi how he could rid himself of his idle thoughts. 'Don't try', exclaimed the Rabbi, 'you have no other thoughts and you would be left empty; try to acquire, one after the other, a few useful thoughts and they will displace the idle ones.' Does nor this tally with Christ's parable of the seven devils? (Matthew 12.45).

We must learn to look with intelligence, thoughtfully, with realism and sobriety and also with live interest, at the complex material which we represent in order to discern all its actual and future potential. But this requires courage and faith. Perhaps you remember the touching and heart-rending phrase of young St Vincent de Paul: 'O God, I am too ugly for human beings, perhaps you have a use for me?' We are all ugly but we are all dear to God who has faith in us. Would he otherwise have taken the risk of calling into existence for all eternity—not for a passing moment —each one of us?

At every instant of our lives we can be authentic and real if we choose the risk of being what we are and of not aiming at copying a model or identifying ourselves with preconceived images. But our true self cannot be discovered merely by watching our empirical self, but only in God and through him. Each of us is an image of the Living God, but an image which, like an old painting that has been tampered with, overlaid or clumsily restored to the point of being unrecognisable, yet in which some features of the original survive; a specialist can scrutinise it and, starting with what is still genuine, clean the whole painting of all its successive additions. St Paul advises us to find ourselves in Christ and Christ in us; instead of attaching ourselves to what is wrong, ugly and sinful, to learn to see what is already in the image of God and, having discovered it, to remain faithful to our own truest and best self. Instead of asking ceaselessly the question 'what is wrong with me?' why not ask ourselves the question 'in what way am I already akin to God? in harmony with him? How far am I on the way of reaching the full measure of the stature of Christ?' Would not that be more inspiring in our striving for perfection?

We are encompassed on all sides by worries, concerns, fears and desires and so inwardly perturbed that we hardly ever live within ourselves—we live beside ourselves. We are so much in a state of befuddlement that it takes either acts of God or a deliberate discipline to come to our senses and begin that inward journey which will lead us *through* ourselves to God himself. God tries without ceasing to call us back, to open the door of our inner cell. His love, wise and far-sighted, may seem ruthless to us at times, for does not the guardian angel of Hermas say to him: 'Be of good cheer, Hermas, God will not abandon you before He breaks either your heart or your bones!' We seldom perceive God's mercy when it is expressed to us through illness, bereavement or loneliness, and yet how often it is the only way in which God can put an end to the inner and outer turmoil which carries us away like a flood! How often do we exclaim 'If only I had a short period of peace, if only something made me aware that life had greatness, that eternity exists!' and God sends us such moments when we are brought up short by illness or accident; but instead of understanding that the hour of recollection, of withdrawal and of renewal has come, we fight desperately to return as fast as possible to our former state, rejecting the gift concealed in that act of God which frightens us. And when bereavement comes to us, instead of growing and becoming as great as life and death, we shrink into selfcentredness and self-pity and lose sight of the eternity into which we could enter together with the one who, as St Paul says, 'is now clothed with eternity'.

However, even the ability to use and take advantage of God-given circumstances requires an inner and outer discipline and an enlightened faith capable of discerning God's path. Such a vision does not imply that we are entitled to charge God himself with all that goes wrong with the world. Indeed, according to ancient Christian teaching, three wills contend for the fate of the world. The will of God, wise, loving, free, capable of acting with sovereign power, inexorably patient; the will of Satan and the powers of darkness, always evil and yet powerless to reach into the souls of men; the will of fallen man, uncertain, wavering between the call of God and the beguilements of the devil, endowed with the dread power of freedom to choose between God and the Adversary, between life and death, between good and evil.

When we think of spiritual discipline we usually think in terms of rules of life, rules of thinking and meditation, rules of prayers, which are aimed at drilling us into what we imagine to be the pattern of a real Christian life. But when we observe people who submit themselves to that kind of strict discipline, and when we ourselves attempt this, we usually see that the results are far less than we would expect. And this generally comes from the fact that we take the means for the end, that we concentrate so much on the means that we never achieve the end at all, or that we achieve them to so small a degree that it was not worth putting in all that effort to achieve so little. This results, I believe, from not understanding what spiritual discipline is and what it is aimed at.

We must remember that discipline is not the same thing as drill. Discipline is a word connected with the word 'disciple'. Discipline is the condition of the disciple, the situation of the disciple with regard both to his master and to what he is learning. And if we try to understand what discipleship means when it is put into action, when it results in discipline, we may easily find the following things. First of all, discipleship means a sincere desire to learn and a determination to learn at all cost. I know that the words 'at all cost' may mean a great deal more for one person than for another. It depends on the zeal and the conviction or the longing we have for the learning. Yet it is always 'at all cost' for this particular person. A sincere desire to learn is not so often to be discovered in our hearts. Quite often we wish to learn up to a point, provided

14

the effort will not be too great, provided we have guarantees that the final result will be worth the effort. We do not launch into this learning whole-heartedly enough and this is why so often we do not achieve what we could achieve. So the first condition if we wish to become disciples fruitfully and learn a discipline which will give results, is integrity of purpose. This is not easily acquired.

We must also be ready to pay the cost of discipleship. There is always a cost to discipleship because, from start to finish, it means a gradual overcoming of all that is self in order to grow into communion with that which is greater than self and which will ultimately displace self, conquer the ground and become the totality of life. And there is always a moment in the experience of discipleship when fear comes upon the disciple, for he sees at a certain moment that death is looming, the death that his self must face. Later on it will no longer be death, it will be a life greater than his own, but every disciple will have to die first before he comes back to life. This requires determination, courage, faith.

This being said, discipleship begins with silence and listening. When we listen to someone we think we are silent because we do not speak; but our minds con- tinue to work, our emotions react, our will responds for or against what we hear, we may even go further than this, with thoughts and feelings buzzing in our heads which are quite unrelated to what is being said. This is not silence as it is implied in discipleship. The real silence towards which we must aim as a starting point, is a complete repose of mind and heart and will, the complete silence of all there is in us, including our body, so that we may be completely aware of the word we are receiving, completely alert and yet in complete repose. The silence I am speaking of is the silence of the sentry on duty at a critical moment; alert, immobile, poised and yet alive to every sound, every movement. This living silence is what discipleship requires first of all, and this is not achieved without effort. It requires from us a training of our attention, a training of our body, a training of our mind and our emotions so that they are kept in check, completely and perfectly.

The aim of this silence is the perceiving of what will be offered us, of the word that will resound in the silence. And this word we must be prepared to hear, whatever it may be. This requires a moral, intellectual integrity, because very often we listen hoping that we shall hear what we wish to hear and ready at the very moment we do not hear the right words, to switch off our understanding or our attention in order not to hear; or else we switch on the sinister ability we have to misunderstand, to misinterpret, to understand in our way what is spoken in God's way. Here again training in moral and intellectual integrity is essential. Then when we listen, we shall hear; we may hear dimly or clearly, we may hear all we need to know or, to begin with, just enough for us to have a clue, to pay more attention, to learn more about silence and about listening. But in order to hear we must be prepared to receive any word which will be spoken to us, and in order to understand we must be prepared to do whatever God commands.

This leads me to another point in this process of learning spiritual discipline. If we are satisfied with simply listening in interest, without ever doing what we are told, quite soon we shall hear nothing any more. God does not speak to our mind or to our heart if he does not receive allegiance and obedience from us. God speaks once and he speaks twice, says a passage in the Old Testament, and then, as a modern writer puts it, he withdraws sadly until we are hungry for God, hungry for the truth, hungry enough to be ready to receive any word, which is the Bread of Life. The determination to *do* is essential in this life of spiritual discipline.

When the Lord Christ spoke to his disciples and to the crowds that surrounded him, he did not deliver a general teaching to be received by all in the terms he was using. Part of his teaching had a universal meaning, but part of those words of Christ which are recorded in the Gospel were spoken to one particular man in one particular situation. This man had to receive them as the word of God, because they were addressed to him. Others in the crowd might not have found in them an answer to their question. We must be attentive, when we read the Gospels, to those passages which first of all apply to us directly, in order to become doers of the will of God. There are passages in the Gospel which we understand intellectually; other passages which we do not understand. There are passages against which we rebel; there are passages which, in the words of St Luke, 'make our hearts burn within us'. These words, these passages, these images or commandments, are spoken to us directly. We may assume that here the Lord Christ and we are of the same mind, understand one another, that these words of Christ tell us of what we already know from experience of life, and those are absolute commandments. Those words we must never forget. We must apply those words in our life at every moment. Whenever we fail to do so we break our relationship with Christ, we turn away, we refuse the burden, the yoke of his discipleship.

Doing the will of God is a discipline in the best sense of the word. It is also a test of our loyalty, of our fidelity to Christ. It is by doing in every detail, at every moment, to the utmost of our power, as perfectly as we can, with the greatest moral integrity, using our intelligence, our imagination, our will, our skill, our experience, that we can gradually learn to be strictly, earnestly obedient to the Lord God. Unless we do this our discipleship is an illusion and all our life of discipline, when it is a set of self-imposed rules in which we delight, which makes us proud and self-satisfied, leaves us nowhere, because the essential momentum of our discipleship is the ability in this process of silence and listening, to reject our self, to allow the Lord Christ to be our mind, our will and our heart. Unless we renounce ourselves and accept his life in place of our life, unless we aim at what St Paul defines as 'it is no longer I but Christ who lives in me', we shall never be either disciplined or disciples.

This effort that leads us to overcome our self, to kill in us the old Adam so that the new Adam may live in us, is not only achieved in our actions, in our doing what the Gospel says. One of the writers of the early church, Mark the Ascetic, says that 'no-one will ever have fulfilled the will of God in his actions if this will he has not fulfilled in his heart', because it is the heart of man, it is the inner man who must be transformed. We are not called to ape the Lord Christ, to imitate him outwardly. We are called to become inwardly what he is, to have with him a communion of life, a common life in the mysterious body which is his Church. And we must therefore overcome the old Adam in our thought and in our heart and in our will. In our will we overcome the old Adam by acting according to the imperatives of the Gospel; but in our mind and heart the struggle is far deeper and more difficult. We must mould our minds and hearts so that we should have the mind of Christ—meditation on the Gospel, to grasp with intellectual integrity what the Lord said, in all truth, and not what we wish him to have said; the ability by an effort of moral integrity to see that these words of God judge us and lead us into a greater measure of truth.

The same is true when we choose words of prayer. So often we say, why pray in words coined by others? Do not my own words express adequately what is in my heart and mind? No, this is not enough. Because what we aim at is not simply to express lyrically what we are, what we have learned, what we wish. In the same way in which we learn from the great masters of music and of art what musical or artistic beauty is, so also do we learn from those masters of the spiritual life, who have achieved what we aim at, who have become real, live and worthy members of the Body of Christ; from them we must learn how to pray, to find those dispositions, those attitudes of mind, of will and of heart which make us Christians. This again is an act of rejection of our own self, to allow something greater and truer than our self to live in us, to give us shape and impetus and direction.

These are the main elements of spiritual discipline. It is a road, a way in which we open ourselves to Christ, to the grace of God. This is all discipline, all we can do. It is God who in response to this ascetical endeavour will give us his grace and fulfil us. We have a tendency to think that what we are to aim at is a high, deep, mystical life. This is not what we should aim at. A mystical life is a gift from God; in itself it is not an achievement of ours and even less is it an expression of our devotion to God. What we must aim at in response to the love of God declared, manifest in Christ, is to become true disciples by bringing ourselves as a sacrifice to God; on our part it is the ascetical endeavour which is the summit of our loyalty, allegiance and love. We must offer this to God and he will fulfil all things as he has promised. 'My child, give me thy heart; I shall fulfil all things.'

We are now ready to start; to reflect on the way already trodden, the experience already gained and the journey which lies ahead of us. The life of each of us is to be in a sense a quest of the grail. Let us then

take unto us the whole armour of God; stand therefore, having our loins girt about with truth, and
having on the breastplate of righteousness; and our
feet shod with the preparation of the gospel of
peace; above all, taking the shield of faith and the
helmet of salvation, and the sword of the spirit,
which is the word of God.

Ephesians 6.13–17

We shall follow a path traced by centuries of Christian
pilgrims, taking as landmarks for our meditation
certain passages of the Gospel. At the close of our
journey, we ought to be able to forget ourselves so that
we can enter into a vision which transcends us, and at
the same time leads us to the complete trust that alone
can bring us to a true conversion, to a return towards
the Lord, to the beginning of a new relationship with
him, to our coming home.

THE JOURNEY

The Story of Bartimaeus

And they came to Jericho; and as he went out of Jericho with his disciples and a great number of people, blind Bartimaeus, the son of Timaeus, sat by the highway side, begging. And when he heard that it was Jesus of Nazareth, he began to cry out, and say, 'Jesus, thou son of David, have mercy on me.' And many charged him that he should hold his peace; but he cried the more a great deal, 'Thou son of David, have mercy on me.' And Jesus stood still, and commanded him to be called, and they called the blind man, saying to him, be of good comfort, rise; he calleth thee. And he, casting away his garment, rose, and came to Jesus. And Jesus answered and said unto him, 'What wilt thou that I should do unto thee?' The blind man said unto Him, 'Lord, that I might receive my sight.' And Jesus said unto him: 'Go thy way; the faith hath made thee whole.' And immediately he received his sight, and followed Jesus in the way.

Mark 10.46–52

I BELIEVE that one of the reasons which prevent us from being truly ourselves and finding our own way is that we do not realise the extent to which we are blind! If only we knew that we were blind, how eagerly would we seek healing: we should seek it, as Bartimaeus probably did, from men, doctors, priests, healers; and then, having lost all hope 'in princes, in the sons of men in whom there is no salvation', we might, perhaps, turn to God. But the tragedy is that we do not realise our blindness: too many things leap to our eyes for us to be aware of the invisible to which we are blind. We live in a world of things which command our attention and assert themselves: we have no need to affirm them, they are *there*. Things invisible do not assert themselves—we have to seek them out and discover them. The outside world demands our attention: God entreats us diffidently. I recall an old monk who said to me: 'The Holy Spirit is like a great shy bird which has alighted a little way off. When you see It coming closer, don't move, don't frighten It, let It come up to you.' That may perhaps make us think of the descent of the Holy Spirit in the shape of a dove. This image of a bird flying down, shy and, at the same time, ready to give itself, is scriptural and full of meaning—although a Japanese once said to me: 'In the Christian religion I think I understand about the Father and the Son, but I can never discover the significance of the honourable bird!'

To continue for a moment in the world of symbols of timidity, of a heart which bestows but never prostitutes itself, have another look at the passage in *The Little Prince* by Antoine de Saint-Exupéry where the fox describes how the little prince should learn to tame him—he must be very patient, sit a little way off and look at him out of the corner of his eye and say nothing, for words cause misunderstandings. And every day he will sit a little closer and they will become friends. Put 'God' in the place of the fox and you will see loving, chaste shyness, a diffidence which offers but does not prostitute itself: God does not accept a glib, smooth relationship, nor does he impose his presence—he offers it, but it can only be received on the same terms, those of a humble, loving heart, of two, timidly, shyly seeking each other because of deep mutual respect and because both recognise the holiness and the extraordinary beauty of reciprocal love.

The outside world asserts itself. The world within can be sensed but it never clamours for attention. We must step gently, carefully: we must watch for the inner world like a bird-watcher who takes up a position in the woods or the fields silent, yet vibrating with life; he, too, quiet, alert and watchful. This attentive attitude which allows us to perceive what otherwise escapes our awareness could be described in the words of this old nursery rhyme:

> A wise old owl lived in an oak,
> The more he saw the less he spoke.
> The less he spoke the more he heard;
> Why can't we all be like that bird?

Blinded by the world of things we forget that it does not match the depth of which man is capable. Man is both small and great. When we think of ourselves in an ever-expanding universe—immeasurably big or infin ly small—we see ourselves as a speck of dust, ent, frail, of no account; but when we turn inwards we discover that nothing in this immensity is great enough to fill us to the brim—the whole created world falls like a grain of sand into the depth of our being: we are too vast for it to fill or fulfil us. God alone, who has made us for himself, on his scale, can do that. In the words of Angelus Silesius:

> I am as great as God,
> He is as small as I.

The world of things has an opacity, a density, weight and volume, but it has no depth. We can always penetrate to the heart of things, and when we have reached their deepest point, it is a terminal point, there is no way through to infinity: the centre of a sphere is its innermost point but if we try to go beyond that we return to the surface at the antipodes. But Holy Scripture speaks of the depth of the human heart. It is not a depth that can be measured; its very nature is immensity, it goes beyond all bounds of measurement. This depth is rooted in the immensity of God himself. It is only when we have understood the difference between a presence that asserts itself and a presence we have to seek because we sense it in our hearts, when we have understood the difference between the heavy, opaque density of the world around us and the human profundity which only God can fill—and I would go so far as to say the profundity of every created thing whose vocation it is to become the place of the divine presence, when, all things accomplished, God will be all in all things—it is only then that we can begin our search in the knowledge that we are blind, blinded by the visible which prevents us grasping the invisible.

To be blind to the invisible, to be aware only of the tangible world, is to be on the outside of the fullness of knowledge, outside the experience of total reality which is the world in God and God at the heart of the world. The blind man Bartimaeus was painfully aware of this because owing to his physical blindness, the visible world escaped him. He could cry out to the Lord in utter despair, with all the desperate hope he felt when salvation was passing him by, because he felt himself cut off. The reason why all too often we cannot call to God in this way is that we do not realise how much we are cut off by being blind to the total vision of the world—a vision which could afford complete reality to the visible world itself. If only we could learn to be blind to the visible in order to see beyond, in depth, the invisible, in and around us, penetrating all things with its presence!

Blindness is manifold: it may, never with us, but with the saints, result from having seen a light too bright. St Symeon the New Theologian, speaking of the Divine Darkness, says that it is excess of light, of a light so blinding that he who has seen it, sees no more. It may also be blindness with open eyes. Tolstoy, in *War and Peace*, tells of Pierre Bezuhov who looks into the big, beautiful eyes of Helen and sees in them nothing but himself, free from all faults, as she (poor thing) saw him. He looked into her eyes and saw only himself—missed her completely! We do that too, even in the world of things; according to the way we focus our eyes when we look at a window, we may see our reflection, or the pane of glass, or the view beyond. We can see with the eyes of indifference as the passers-by saw Bartimaeus. We can see with the eyes of greed as the glutton in Dickens who, seeing cattle grazing in the fields, could only think 'live beef!' We can see with the eyes of hatred when we become horribly clear-sighted but with the perspicacity of the devil, seeing nothing but evil, making a vile caricature of things. And lastly, we may see with the eyes of love, with a pure heart that can see God and his image in people; even in those where his image is dimmed— through layers of appearances and counter evidence, to the true, deep secret self of man. For it is as the fox tells the little prince: 'We can see truly only with the heart, what is vital is invisible to the eye.'

We must recognise that we are not conscious of the depth of things, the immensity, the vocation of eternity of the whole world and we can only become aware of this in so far as, by some primordial experience, we are certain that there exists an inner world; and it is through faith that we can stand fast in the certainty that the invisible is real, present and worthy of being sought for, beyond, through and at the very heart of the visible. This act of faith means accepting the witness of those who are aware of the invisible world, even if we only take it as a working hypothesis, a temporary one perhaps, to permit of investigation. Without that, nothing is possible—we cannot set out in search of the invisible if *a priori* we are sure that it does not exist. We can accept the witness, not of one or two people, but of millions who, in the course of history, in Christian and non-Christian religions alike, have experienced the invisible and have witnessed to its presence.

Then we must, I think, enlarge our field of vision and our understanding of life in general. I believe that in our day we still live under the illusion that everything that is not rational is dubious. And yet psychology has shown us that there is a whole irrational world that is decisive in a man's inner life. When I say 'irrational' I do not mean 'unreasonable'. There is, for instance, the entire range of human love, whether it be friendship, family love, the love that singles out from the crowd the one who is unique for us, who re-orientates the whole world for us. As one of the old Greek writers said: 'Before a man meets and loves the girl who will be his betrothed, he is surrounded by men and women; from the moment he discovers the beloved—it is *she* and the others are people.' This experience, so rich, so complex and so universal, belongs to the order of the irrational in the sense that it cannot be manufactured by reason: to love someone is not a balance sheet of reasons for and against; it is a direct experience, a fact which imposes itself but which goes too deep for us to be able to speak of any reasoned argument. It is the same with the experience of beauty, whether it be in music or the plastic arts, whether it depend on the ear or the eye; it is not just the sum total of good reasons for admiring a work of art. If we wish to share with someone our experience of the beauty of a piece of music, of sculpture, of architecture or of painting we begin by inviting them with the words Christ spoke to his first disciples: 'Come and see!' We certainly would not begin by saying: 'First I am going to explain to you all the beauty in this work of art, and when you understand it properly, then you can be allowed to experience it.'

In these two primordial experiences of love and beauty, we find ourselves confronted with someone or something which may have gone unperceived for years or never before noticed. For some reason, suddenly, unaccountably, we see what we have not seen before. In a group of people, a girl and a young man are part of the crowd. And then one day they see each other. Something happens, like a ray of sunshine falling on stained glass. The glass, without sunlight, looks like a criss-cross of darker lines on an uneven grey background. Suddenly there is illumination, beauty, theme, sense. Now one sees the stained glass. The ray of sunlight is ephemeral, it will be extinguished at the end of the day or in a moment, but whoever saw the window now knows that it is not a grey patch but a stained glass window which has become invisible. Certainty prevails over the evidence: this is what we call faith. I know that all the beauty I have perceived is there although it seems to be quenched.

Now, there are two ways of regarding this window, given the fact that I have once seen it. The window, like all revelations, is a two-fold revelation: it is revealed by the ray of sunshine which lit it up and it reveals the ray of sunshine which, without it, would have remained invisible. Two people meet and see each other illuminated, so to speak, from within, revealed to each other by the light of the grace of God, in all the splendour of their reality, such as God sees them. These two people can, when the splendour dies, preserve the certainty of it and remember that the vision was given them just because God irradiated the depths and showed them. But what happens more often is that, having seen someone in the splendour of this glory, we forget the vision which has been given to us by a light from beyond and, foolishly, we imagine that all the beauty belonged to the person himself. What was stained glass becomes an idol, what was revelation becomes an opaque wall beyond which we cannot see. You know very well—all literature speaks of it—how a fleeting vision can be transformed afterwards into an idolatry which is labelled passionate love and is the subject of the romances of every country.

Until we learn that we must preserve the vision we have had in the richness of a two-fold co-relative relation; as long as we continue to transform into idols all that God reveals to us of human or artistic beauty, we shall be transforming what should be an opportunity of revelation into one of not seeing any more, because we have changed the girl we love into an idol; or having seen a tree against the sky in a loveliness that had never struck us before, it is the tree we worship instead of realising the whole complex of things and events which has revealed something we had not grasped before. While we do this we shall never know, even on the simplest, most natural, most human plane, a new dimension and we shall go on living in two dimensions, time and space. We must accept to the utmost the experience of loving, cherish and discover the beauty of things and of people. Then, when we have discovered on this plane the dimension which goes beyond reason, which can be examined by the reason but not created by it, we shall be much nearer to making discoveries bearing on God.

The instant we realise we are blind and therefore outside the Kingdom, we can occupy in relation to the Kingdom and to God, a situation which is real—not the imaginary one in which we constantly place ourselves, outside in the street, picturing the eternal abode, trying to warm our hands at the fire burning in the hearth on the other side of the door, endeavouring here and now to share in the life which is still out of our reach, imagining already that the tiny spark which shines in us is even now all the Kingdom. It is not yet the Kingdom, it is only an earnest pledge of life eternal, a promise, an appeal lodged in us to make us continue in hope as we take our stand where the Gospel tells us to begin—before a door which is still shut to us, never wearying of knocking at it until it opens. We must hold ourselves before the mystery not yet penetrated and call, cry out towards God, seeking the way until it unfolds before us like a straight path to heaven, in the certainty that the moment will come when God will grant our prayer. I purposely do not say 'hear' because we are always heard although a perceptible response is not always given to us. God is not deaf to our prayers but we are not always capable of understanding God's silence in response to our cry. If we realised we were outside a closed door, we could measure both our human solitude and also how far we still are from the joy to which we are called, from the fullness which God offers us, and we could at the same time appreciate—and this is very important—how rich we are despite our infinite poverty. We know so little of the things of God, we live so little in him yet what wealth there is for us in this spark of Presence, of knowledge, of communion shining at the heart of the darkness that we are! If the darkness is yet so rich in light, if absence is so rich in presence, if life which but dawns is such fullness, with what hope, with what mounting joy, can we stand before this closed door, in the happy thought that one day it will open and we shall know an outburst of life such as we cannot yet contain within ourselves.

We do not need always to seek the presence of God in a perceptible way; we do not need to hope every moment that God will reveal himself to us discernibly. The Gospels offer us a certain number of examples which show how far we are from understanding the holiness, the majesty of God; how little we marvel at God, and therefore find it so natural to look for his presence, whereas in reality we ought shyly, hoping for the impossible, ask God to transform, to convert us, before we hope to find ourselves in his awesome presence, since every encounter with God, to a greater or lesser degree, is already the last judgement: to find oneself face to face with the living God is something of grave, of fateful consequence. To meet God is always a 'crisis' and in Greek the word 'crisis' means 'judgement'. We can present ourselves before God and either

35

be condemned or saved, according to what we bring in our hearts and in the testimony of our lives. That is why the prophets of the Old Testament—and one could quote many instances—used to lament: 'Alas, woe is me, I have seen God, and shall die!' It is more than the human soul can bear, unless the human soul, the person, has been grafted on to the very life of God in Christ.

It is rash to seek a premature meeting. That is why the whole teaching of the Orthodox Church, for prayer and conduct of life, tells us: 'Do not seek any mystical experience; ask God in an act of adoration, with all the attention and faith of which you are capable, with all the hope and desire you possess, to change you, to make you such that "one day" you can meet Him.' And this is something deep-rooted in the Gospels: remember the miraculous draught of fishes. Peter has taken Christ into his boat, Christ has been speaking to the crowds in his presence, yet Peter has not perceived his majesty. The Lord tells his disciples to launch out into the deep and let down their nets. Peter answers him: 'We have toiled all night and have taken nothing; nevertheless at thy word I will do as thou sayest.' He lets down his net and cannot pull it up! He asks those in the other boats to help and only then realises once more—but not finally until God himself reveals to him that Christ is the Son of the living God —that he is in the presence of something, of someone, greater than he can conceive of. He is seized with a reverent awe, falls down at Jesus' feet and cries: 'Depart from me, I am a sinful man.' At that moment he has an intuition of the majesty of him who was present among them and, knowing what he himself was, he begged him to depart.

Does it often happen to us, at moments when prayer has gone deep, at moments when we are conscious of God, of his holiness, of his grandeur, to say to him: 'Lord, depart from me, I am unworthy of the nearness which thou hast thyself established'? Do we not more often try to provoke, to force on God a closeness, an intimacy which God has not sought, to impose ourselves on him, to force the door which he sought to keep shut? Remember also the centurion who besought Christ to heal his servant. 'I will come and heal him,' said the Lord. 'No,' answered the centurion. 'Do not trouble thyself, I too am a man under authority, and yet when I tell my servant to do my will, he does it. It is enough for you to speak a word and my servant shall be healed where he is.' Is that our attitude? Do we possess such a sense of God that we do not want to compel him to come? A word is enough, we do not need more. Do we vindicate his sovereign freedom and worship his greatness? Do we know through an inner certainty that his word is life for those to whom it is addressed? If only we realised that because of our blindness we are outside the Kingdom, without the Presence, we could then knock at the door, seek the way, cry to the Lord and not say to him: 'Open at once, I haven't the patience to wait; appear before me now, I have waited too long for thee!' Yet that is precisely what we are always doing. In twenty-four hours we manage to find a short half-hour to devote to the Lord and we are surprised that the moment we say 'In the Name of the Father, the Son and the Holy Spirit' the whole majesty of the Trinity is not revealed to us!

It is of the utmost importance for us to learn both how far we are outsiders and how richly we are already endowed with his presence, by the light enclosed in our darkness; our very potentialities can be an inspiration, a way, a hope; how little we need hurry but how important it is to be real, to occupy in relation to God and to the world around us the true situation which is ours, within which God can act. For he cannot act in an unreal situation, in which we are continually placing ourselves through imagination, fantasy, desire, and spiritual gluttony, as the Fathers of the Desert say.

Then one problem would be solved for us, one aspect of prayer which is a torment in our life would become a creative act, one full of meaning: to pray with a sense of the absence of God, something we so rarely do with a fulfilled heart! How we lament this absence! How little we take advantage of it to become more real and say: 'I am blind, I stand outside the door, I am in the cold and in the dark, not because I am in outer darkness, rejected by God's judgement, but as at the beginning of Genesis at the moment God was creating all things, drawing from darkness light, so that what I called light yesterday is only twilight today.' To pray in the absence of God, to know that he is there but I am blind; that he is there but I am insensitive and it is an act of his infinite mercy not to be present to me while I am not yet capable of sustaining his coming.

If we look carefully at what is at the bottom of this dark labyrinth that is our heart, our consciousness, our past, our present, our impulses towards the future, can we say that we are prepared for a meeting with God? Dare we wish for one? Yes, but only in God's own time, as a gift from him; but to will it and force God to such a meeting—no! It is more than we could bear. And yet that is how we behave, blinded by the visible, sightless before the awesome greatness of the Invisible, lacking that sense of wonder, of reverent fear, of that vision which faith gives of the humbling feeling of having touched the hem of the robe of Christ. If only we could appreciate, could be grateful to God for his absence which teaches us to knock at the door, to test our thoughts and our hearts, to consider the significance of our actions, to appraise the impulses of our whole being, to ask ourselves whether our will is really orientated towards God or if we look to God for a moment's respite from our burdens, only to forsake him the next instant, as soon as we have recovered our strength, to squander that energy he has given us like the prodigal son.

These things are important because unless our point of departure is a realistic one and we are aware of the true nature of things and accept them entirely as a gift from God in response to the situation in which we are, we shall pass our time in trying to force a lock in a door which will open of itself one day. St John Chrysostom tells us: 'Find the key to your heart; you will see that this key will also open the door of the Kingdom.' That is the direction our search should take.

The Parable of the Pharisee and the Publican

And he spake this parable unto certain which trusted in themselves that they were righteous, and despised others: two men went up into the temple to pray; the one a Pharisee, and the other a publican. The Pharisee stood and prayed thus with himself, God, I thank thee, that I am not as other men are, extortioners, unjust, adulterers, or even as this publican. I fast twice in the week, I give tithes of all that I possess. And the publican, standing afar off, would not lift up so much as his eyes unto heaven, but smote his breast, saying, God be merciful to me a sinner. I tell you, this man went down to his house justified rather than the other: for every one that exalteth himself shall be abased; and he that humbleth himself shall be exalted.

Luke 18.9–14

THIS parable confronts us with human and divine judgement. The pharisee walks into the temple and takes his stand before God. He knows he has a right to do so; is not his conduct defined in every detail by the law God himself gave to his people—not to speak of the innumerable regulations which the elders and the pharisees had deduced from it and made the touchstone of piety. The realm of God is his own realm; he belongs to it, he vindicates God's rights, God shall vindicate his. God's realm is that of the law and the man who obeys it, who enlarges it, is surely righteous. He is within the formal Old Testament view of things; the law, in the Old Testament, if obeyed, could make a man righteous within the terms of the Covenant. One thing the law could not do was to give eternal life, for eternal life is to know God and him whom he sent, Jesus Christ (John 17.3), but not from the outside as the pharisee knew him, the Almighty Law-Giver, but within the intimate relation of a common life ('I in you and you in me', John 14.20). The pharisee knows all about action, but nothing about being. In all his life of righteousness there is one thing he has never come across, never perceived: that between God and him there can be a relationship of mutual love. He never sought it and never met the God of Isaiah who is so holy that before him all our righteousness is like a tree blown down by a hurricane. He believes that between God and his creatures there is a relation that is fixed, fossilised, immutable. He has never discerned in the Scriptures the love story of God and the world he created and so loved that he would give his only-begotten Son that it might be saved. He lives within a covenant which he takes for a bargain, without any relationship. Of God he knows the law— not the Person. He has no terms of reference to condemn himself; he is just, cold, dead.

Can we not recognise ourselves in this picture, others too and whole human groups? Here is a short rhyme which brings it out admirably:

> We are the sweet, selected few,
> All others may be damned;
> There's still room in hell for you,
> *We* don't want our heaven crammed!

But the publican knows that he is evil, because both God's law and man's judgement are against him. He transgresses the law of God and uses, manipulates it, for his benefit. He breaks slyly or arrogantly, according to circumstance, the laws of men and uses them to his advantage—and for this he is hated and despised of men. So when he comes, he dares not cross the threshold of the temple, because the temple is the place of the Presence and he has no right, he shrinks from entering into the Presence of God. He stands then and sees this holy space that extends ahead of him, seeming to convey the immensity of God and the infinite distance between him and holiness—God. This temple is as great as the Presence Itself and as frightening, as tragic as the judgement which confrontation between sin and holiness signifies. And from his hard, cruel human experience, emerges that unfathomably deep and authentic prayer 'Lord, have mercy on me a sinner'. What has he learnt of life? He knows that wherever the law is applied without mitigation, there is suffering; that under the unbounded domination of the law there is no mercy. It is the law he uses and abuses to entrap his debtors, to corner his victims, the law which, cunningly handled, will justify him when he will send to prison his insolvent debtors, that law whose power he can count on to accumulate his wealth and possessions, ruthlessly, and without mercy.

And yet, his very human experience has taught him something else, quite illogical and running counter to his outlook on life: he remembers moments in his life and in the lives of others as cruel and merciless as himself, when, perhaps, armed with all the power of the law, he comes face to face with the misery and terror he has inflicted on a family, the suffering of a mother, the tears of a child, and at the very moment when everything is his, to the stunned amazement of his confederates, in spite of the law, in spite of the ruthless logic of his breed, in spite of common sense and habitual behaviour, he stays his hand, and looks around in silence, smiles perhaps sadly or gently and says: 'Let them be!'

He may know too that his life was saved from ruin or bankruptcy, prison or ignominy by an absurd, unaccountable gesture of comradeship, of generosity or pity and that such actions set boundaries to the law of the iniquitous jungle that was his world. Something in him has outgrown the confines of his rigidity; it is these gestures of compassion or solidarity that are the sole hope in a world of evil. So standing outside on the threshold of the temple which he cannot enter, because within the law reigns and justice has dominion, because his doom is written at the heart of things, by the door, he begs for mercy. He asks for no justice—he would have justice suspended. In the sixth century, the great ascetic St Isaac the Syrian wrote: 'Never say that God is just. If He were just you would be in hell. Rely only on His injustice which is mercy, love and forgiveness.'

Such is the publican's situation and what he had learnt about life. How much we can learn from him! Why not, like him, with dim or clear awareness of our sinful state, stand humbly and patiently on the threshold. Can we claim a right to meet God face to face?

Have we any place as we are in God's own realm? If he chooses to come to us, as he did in the Incarnation and in the days of his flesh and throughout human history, to meet us as our Saviour and Redeemer, let us fall down at his feet in wonder and gratitude. In the meanwhile, let us remain at the door and say to the Lord: 'O Lord, if you search our iniquity who shall stand? O Lord, receive me into the Realm of Grace, not into that of justice and retribution!'

Yet we make this action of grace impossible, by reverting to the law, by becoming pharisees—not that we emulate their stern and costly faithfulness to the law of God and the rules of the elders—but by sharing their mentality void of hope and of charity. The pharisee was at least righteous according to the law; we are not even that, though we fancy ourselves worthy to take our stand before God. If we only stopped at the gate and knocked humbly, shyly, and listened for a call to come in, we might discover with wonder and amazement that, on the other side, Someone is also knocking: 'I stand at the door and I knock', says the Lord (Revelation 3.20). We might discover that on his side the door is unlocked; it is on our side that it is locked, it is our heart that is sealed and oh! so narrow, so unwilling to take the *risk* of letting go the law and entering into the realm of love where everything is as frail and as unconquerable as love and life itself. But God goes on knocking with hope, insistence, patience, unceasingly, through people, circumstances and the still, small voice of our conscience, as the beggar knocks at the rich man's door, because, having chosen to be poor, he waits that our love and our charity would open to him a true, human heart. And what he needs to come in and sup with us is that we should reject our heart of stone and acquire a heart of flesh (Ezekiel 11.19); what he offers is forgiveness and freedom.

He seeks from us an encounter: this theme of the encounter is central to the experience of the Christian world, it is also the basis of all the history of salvation, of all human history. It is the centre of the Good News of the New Testament. In the Old Testament, to see God was to die; in the New Testament to meet God is to live. The Christian world today is coming to an ever clearer understanding that all the Gospel can be thought of and should be experienced and lived as an ever-renewed encounter, which embraces both salvation and judgement. Even before the New Testament account, God's first act of creation is an encounter, willed by God, called by God into being; the whole created world emerges out of non-being, and with a sense of primeval wonder discovers both the Creator, the living God, the Giver of life and each one of his creatures and his works. What wonder! what marvel! what joy! Here begins the process of becoming which will—one day—bring us to that abundance of life which St Paul describes as 'God shall be all in all things', when man shall become as St Peter says 'partaker of the divine Nature', share in the nature of God.

First encounter, which is the first step on a road which will lead to an ultimate encounter, not merely face to face, but in a communion, a community of life, a perfect and miraculous union which is our fulfilment.

45

And when man turned away from his Creator, when he found himself alone and orphaned in a world which he had betrayed in betraying God and forsaking his own calling, the mystery of the encounter has gone on, but in a new way; God sent his prophets, his saints, his angels and his judges to remind us of the way which would bring us back to him and to ourselves. And when all things were ready—the major encounter, the encounter *par excellence*, the Great Encounter takes place through the Incarnation when the Son of God becomes the Son of Man; the Word becomes flesh, the fullness of God is revealed through matter itself. Universal, cosmic encounter through which both human history and the whole cosmos are potentially fulfilled.

God has become man, he dwelt in our midst; he could be seen, perceived by human senses, touched. He healed. Words which we now read and repeat were spoken by him and gave life to people. A new life, life eternal. And around him, men and women and children have met one another, undergone an encounter with each other in a way they had never experienced, never even dreamed of. They had seen one another before, but in the presence of the living God they had discovered one another as they had never known before. And this encounter, which is both judgement and salvation, goes on from century to century. As from the beginning, we are in the presence of our God. As in the time of Christ, we stand face to face with a God who willed to become man and, as of old, day in and day out, human beings meet face to face in a completely new way once they have recognized in

Jesus of Nazareth the Son of God and through him have seen the Father. This encounter takes place all the time, but our awareness is so dim that we miss its significance, its immeasurable possibilities and also what it claims from us.

A true encounter is rarely experienced, if you give it its full meaning. People's paths cross, they come up against one another—how many pass us by in the course of a single day without seeing us? And how many are those at whom we look with unseeing eyes, to whom we address neither a look, nor word, nor smile? And yet, every one of those people was a Presence, an image of the living God, whom God may have sent to us with a message or to receive a message from God through us, a word, a gesture, a look of acknowledgement, of compassion, of understanding. To be carried past one another in the street or in life, by the crowd or by chance, is not yet an encounter. We must learn to look and to see—to look attentively, thoughtfully, taking in the features of a face, its expression, the message of a countenance and of the eyes. We must learn, each of us and also in our human groups social, political, racial, national, to see one another in depth, looking patiently, as long as necessary, in order to see who it is who stands before us.

We all belong to human communities which have been separated or opposed to one another for centuries. For hundreds of years at times, we have turned our back, refusing to look into one another's eyes, moving ever farther apart. Then we have stopped; we have turned round to see him who had been our brother and had become a stranger, even an enemy. But we were still too far apart to be able to distinguish his features, much less to see the image of God in him. This is how the pharisee viewed the publican, how nations look at nations, class at class, church at church, individual at individual.

We must start on a real pilgrimage, a long pilgrimage. We are near enough now to be able to look at one another straight in the eyes, reaching beyond the eyes, into the depth of living hearts, observing minds, evaluating deeds, drawing from all this freshly acquired insight thoughtful and careful conclusions as to what was meant, intended and willed by other men, who no less than we ourselves wanted to understand and fulfil the will of God. All this requires a great deal of good-will. It is all too easy to see in the other what repels us, makes strangers of them. It is as easy to see in those who are on our own side nothing but the most attractive qualities.

But how difficult it is to be just. We usually think of justice in terms of attribution or retribution, of allotting to everyone his due, but justice goes farther and claims more, much more, from us. It begins at the moment when I see my neighbour (individual or collective) as different from me, at times irreducibly different, and recognising his total right to be so, accept the fact that he is himself and has no reason to be merely a replica of myself. He is as much God's creature as I am; he was not made in my image but in God's. He is called to be the likeness of God, not to be the likeness of me; and if he seems to me to be very

48

far from being God's like and kin, if he appears to be a repulsive caricature and not an image of God—has he not as much ground to see me likewise? We are all very ugly indeed, and also very miserable and should have such compassionate regard for one another.

But to assert this basic act of justice is fraught with risk and danger. Physical dangers first: to accept those who love us possessively, without being inwardly destroyed and leaving them with the responsibility of our perishing, is difficult enough, but to accept the existence of an adversary, of one who denies and rejects us, of him who would fain blot us out of existence, is a very costly act of justice. Yet it must be performed and this can be done only by charity, that charity—and may I remind you that charity is akin to cherishing, not to grudging almsgiving—which finds ultimate expression, after the Last Supper, in the Garden on the Mount of Olives and in the Cross of Christ. To acknowledge another man's right to be himself, not to resemble me, is the fundamental act of justice, which alone will make it possible for us to look at a man without trying to see and recognise ourselves in him, but to recognise him and beyond yet within him, to discern the Image of the Lord. But this may be more dangerous than we imagine when the recognition may imperil our own existence or our integrity. I will give an example of this. During the Russian Revolution, a young woman was put into prison. Days of solitary confinement, nights of interrogation, followed. During one of these nights she felt that her strength was failing her, her fortitude and her readiness to stand the test

49

were weakening, and of a sudden she felt hatred and anger welling up in her heart. She wanted to look up at her interrogator, challenge him with all the violence she could muster to break the spell of these endless, hopeless nights of torture, even if she should die for it. She looked up indeed, but she said nothing, because, on the other side of the table, she saw a man as completely exhausted as she was, ashen, worn out, with the same expression of despair and distress on his face, and suddenly she realised that they were not, properly speaking, enemies. Yes, they were sitting on two opposite sides of the table, they were in an irreconcilable tension and opposition, and yet they were both captives of the same historical tragedy, caught up in the same whirlwind of history that had thrown one in one direction and the other in another; neither was free, both were victims. And at that moment she realised, because she saw in the other man a victim like herself, that he also was a human being, not simply a function. He was not an enemy, he was a fellow being, caught up together with her, inseparable from her, in the tragedy. She smiled at the man. That was that act of recognition which is ultimate justice.

But it is not enough to look and to see, we must also learn to listen in order to hear. How often it happens that in a conversation, when opinions differ or clash—while our partner is trying to make us understand his views, opening to us his heart, giving us access to secret and often sacred recesses in his mind—instead of hearing what he says, we glean from his discourse enough material to be ready, the moment he falls silent (if we can wait that long), to contradict him. This is what we mistakenly call a dialogue; the one speaks, the other does not listen. And after the first round one changes places so that in the end each has spoken and none has heard.

So that listening is an art we must learn. It is not words we must hear and judge at their face value; not only phrases we must recognise because we use them ourselves. We must listen with such discernment that we can catch within a phrase, often inadequate, the evanescent gleam of truth, of a thought that struggles to express itself, however dimly, however tentatively; the truth of a heart which strives to make us aware of its treasures and its agony. Alas! all too often we are content with hearing mere words and it is to them that we address our reply. Had we taken the risk of doing more, to be attentive to the tone of voice, we might have discovered that the simplest words were heavy with anguish; we would then be duty-bound to respond to this anguish by compassion, charity, commitment. But how dangerous this is! And so, we choose to listen to words and respond to nothing else, we remain deaf to the spirit and yet 'the letter kills, only the spirit quickens'.

What are we then to do if we want to learn to see and to hear? The first condition was stated above: we must recognise and accept the alterity of the other; the other is different from me and is entitled to be such, I have no right to resent it or to expect him to become like me. But to see him as he is I must come near enough to discern everything there is to be seen, yet not

51

so close as not to see any more the 'wood for the trees'. An image may help us understand this: when we wish to see a statue we take our stand at a definite distance from it. This distance is not the same for everyone; it will depend on whether we see well or not, whether we are short- or long-sighted, but each person will have to find that point in space which will allow him, and perhaps him alone, to see best both the whole and every relevant detail, the point of equipoise between remoteness or closeness. If the distance increases we shall no longer see a statue but a block of stone which will become more and more shapeless as we move away from it. If on the contrary, we come too close, details will acquire undue prominence, and as we come even closer they also will fade away to leave us with nothing but the texture of the stone. Nothing will be left in either case of the message which the statue was to convey to us.

It is in a similar way that we must learn to see one another: to be far enough, to distance ourselves sufficiently to be free from irrational, self-centred reactions, from prejudice, from all those errors of judgement which come with emotional entanglement; yet near enough to feel related, responsible, committed. This will require an effort of will and genuine denying of self. It is easy to relate harmoniously to a statue. It is much more arduous to distance ourselves from a person we love or to come close to someone who is repellent to us. To do this, to conquer both fear and greed, we must disengage ourselves from our egotism, unlearn to see all things as though we were at the centre of the universe. We must learn to see things in an objective manner, as facts, which we can take in and investigate without asking first: how does the person or this circumstance affect me, my well-being, my security, my very existence?; to be so dispassionate as to be able to see through appearances and despite material evidence, in depth, as Christ did—remember the calling of Matthew, the despised tax-gatherer. How different Christ's way is to our own horrible gift of seeing through layers of transparency, of translucence and of light, the equivocal twilight of human imperfection or the darkness of a still unenlightened but rich internal chaos. We are not content to judge actions without giving people the benefit of the doubt; we question their very motives, suspect their intentions, instead of 'believing all things, hoping all things'.

We must act ruthlessly against this tendency we have to judge everything from the viewpoint of our little self. The first step on the way into the Kingdom is defined by Christ as 'deny thyself'. We could put it in harsher terms: when we see that once again, instead of seeing or hearing someone, we are wrapped up in ourselves, we must round on this obstrusive 'I' and cry out in anger: 'Get thee behind me, Satan (Satan in Hebrew means adversary), you think not of the things of God! Out of my way, I'm tired of seeing your face!' The publican knew he was evil in the eyes of God and in the judgement of men, he instinctively knew how to look away from himself, because there was little enjoyment to be gained from contemplating his ugliness. The pharisee could look complacently at himself because, at least in his own mind, righteousness and his person coincided exactly and he saw the law of God mirrored perfectly in his life. He could delight quite sincerely in this vision, marvel in the perfect achievement of the divine wisdom he thought he was. My pious reader, do not be too quick to laugh at him or to express your righteous indignation! Ask yourself whether you are so different from him: you the good churchman, you the law-abiding citizen, you the dutiful member of your conventional society!

To see oneself as the 'adversary', the only thing that stands in God's way, takes more than a passing thought; this kind of awareness is won through daring and generous endeavour: 'Shed your blood and God will give you the Spirit', says of one the Fathers of the Desert. Yet this is exactly God's way with us: He willed us into being. He created us in all the radiance of innocence and purity, and when we had betrayed both him and the whole created world, forfeited our own calling, turned away from him and treacherously delivered the Creation into 'the power of the Prince of this world', he accepted the new situation, accepted us as we had become and the world as we had deformed it. It is he who became man, to be the Christ crucified, rejected by men, because he stood for God, and endured the dereliction of the Cross, because he stood for man. This was how God responded to man's challenge; he accepted us in an act of justice that was infinitely far from our ideas of retribution, he proclaims our right to be ourselves but, knowing how foolish it was for us to choose death instead of life,

Satan instead of him, he chose to become a man among men that we might become gods, to graft us on to the living vine, the living olive tree (Romans 11.16).

He knew moreover how to listen. We see throughout the Gospels *how* Christ listens, how he sees, how he espies and discovers in the crowd the one who needs him or who is ready to respond to his appeal. See how perfectly he involves himself and accepts total commitment, the terrible commitment of the Crucifixion, of our death. And also how free he remains, sovereign, always himself, whatever the stresses, the exigencies, the risks and the cost—setting fearlessly God's absolute claim on us; that we must live and be possessed of Eternal Life.

Let us not leave unnoticed the fact the Christ knows each one of us and takes us as we are—and pays the price for our doings, in order to open to us the Gates of Eternal Life. He said to his disciples at the Last Supper: 'I have given you an example, that ye should do as I have done to you' (John 13.15). Is not this the first thing to do? Can we not hear the apostle call us to 'receive one another as Christ received us'? The pharisee might have looked at the publican within the presence of God and seeing himself condemned, might have discovered a brother in the man he so despised. But he was unaware of his encounter with God—how could he stand in awe, how could he see the other, recognise his neighbour, indeed, God's image in him, when he had no vision of God—the Archetype.

From time to time we see and recognise one another in a revealing moment of distress or joy but, like the pharisee, we cross a threshold, our insight fades and when we meet the brother or the sister we recognised, we see again a stranger, undoing all their hopes. What a world of difference in the spirit of St Paul: 'I have an intolerable sorrow, an unceasing torment in my heart: I wish I could be *cast out* of the presence of Christ myself' that the whole of Israel might be saved.

The Story of Zacchaeus

Jesus entered and passed through Jericho. And, behold, there was a man named Zacchaeus, which was the chief among the publicans, and he was rich. And he sought to see Jesus who he was; and could not for the press, because he was little of stature, and he ran before, and climbed up into a sycamore tree to see him; for he was to pass that way. And when Jesus came to the place, he looked up, and saw him, and said unto him, 'Zacchaeus, make haste, and come down; for today I must abide at thy house.' And he made haste, and came down, and received him joyfully. And when they saw it, they all murmured, saying, that he was gone to be guest with a man that is a sinner. And Zacchaeus stood and said unto the Lord; 'Behold, Lord, the half of my goods I give to the poor; and if I have taken any thing from any man by false accusation, I restore him fourfold.' And Jesus said unto him, 'This day is salvation come to this house, forsomuch as he also is a son of Abraham. For the Son of man is come to seek and to save that which was lost.'

Luke 19.1–10

I SHOULD like to pick out three points from the story of Zacchaeus, stressing one of them particularly.

Zacchaeus is desperately anxious to see Christ. This longing on the part of the publican is witness to the fact that, in spite of a life that is unworthy of the law of God, unworthy of him as a man, he had preserved at the bottom of his heart a feeling for what is true, beautiful, for the human measure of things, and because of this he is capable of meeting with the divine measure of things. And in this passionate wish of his to see Christ face to face he comes up against two difficulties: he is a small man and for this reason he must find a way of catching the eye of the Lord, and this way will make him an object of derision. He is a small man; he will have to climb a tree.

Are we not all very small men? Eclipsed in a crowd and prevented from seeing? Do we not all at some time or other have to raise ourselves to a height which is not ours: go above ourselves while still remaining as small and as poor as we were at the beginning, and do we not also on the occasions when we try to be taller than we are in order to find ourselves face to face with God, risk giving rise to astonishment and mockery? Derision, mockery is generally what stops us more emphatically than anything else in our quest for God. To be harshly criticised, to be attacked head on, to be disliked, shunned and rejected—our pride, our obstinacy and our desire to assert ourselves will stand up to all that. But it is very difficult to bear mockery and laughter. This is the main problem that I should like to consider.

But first let me indicate the third point in the story of Zacchaeus. When Christ goes into Zacchaeus' house, he is received with reverence and joy—this regard for God, this joy in the presence of God is made manifest in Zacchaeus' life by his true conversion, by an act of repentance and *metanoia* which means a completely new direction for his life. Because he has met

God, because this encounter has awakened life and joy in him, because his crippled soul has expanded so that he can be truly human, with all the depth of a human soul at peace with God, Zacchaeus spurns his past. He is ready to right all wrongs, he is anxious to start a new life, free of the past, in an act of trust in God, in a act of faith. It is all this that Christ recognises when he says: 'He also is a son of Abraham'—he belongs to the race of those who could believe, not in an act of credulity but in an act of total engagement. This is why 'salvation is come unto this house'.

But the whole situation hinges on something which might have broken Zacchaeus—the laughter of the crowd. The Fathers of the Church are very insistent on this fact: they tell us that it is not often the attraction of the evil to which we are accustomed, or the opposition we shall encounter, that prevents us from starting a new life—it is the fear of ridicule. I want to elaborate this point. I am a prison chaplain. I remember a man saying to me: 'You don't know how lucky you are, when you want to change your life, to be caught and held up to shame. I tried several times to give up stealing and each time had been got at by my mates scoffing. "Want to set yourself up do you? Want to lose your freedom as a man who has chosen to be alone against a rotten society?"' The day he was caught and put in prison, the day when his friends no longer had a hold on him and society discovered him for what he was, he felt he could start anew. Before, every time he made an effort to change, honest men who did not know that he was a thief, said to themselves: 'What's happening to him? He's changing, but if he's changing, what *was* wrong with him?' Afraid of being discovered, frightened that the bad in him would be revealed just because the good was beginning to dawn, he was glad to be unmasked for he felt that he was now free to change, there was nothing to hide, he could now become a new man.

This fear of the judgement, of the opinions of other men is what so often prevents us from changing, even when we are quite capable of altering, of taking a step, because this step betrays our past. We are far more afraid of being laughed at than of harsh censure.

Imagine the scene. Here is a rich man, with the same sort of status as a bank manager in a small town, wanting to see Christ. He slips into the crowd; he is already a rather quaint figure, being so short. He climbs a tree. Can you imagine the manager of the local bank climbing a tree in the main square, just to see a vagrant prophet? Of course he was beset by catcalls, whistling, jeers and laughter. That was probably the hardest test of his faith. To become the disciple of Christ, to be cast off by one's friends and family for that reason, is a noble act, but to climb a tree like a street urchin when one is a local notability, is something altogether different and much harder! This is what so often prevents us from following Christ: that first step which is going to make us a laughing-stock. 'Are you, a free thinker, to become the slave of outmoded thought? Are you who thought you had the right to do just as you please, to hurl insults in the face of God, to become his slave? You were never afraid of what men would say, are you now turning fearful and going submissively to obey the law?' Can we not hear our own friends comment on our conversion?

There are only two ways of overcoming this vanity, this deference to public opinion: pride or humility. There is no third solution. It was vanity that made Zacchaeus a small man and makes us also small before both God and man. Vanity has two particular characteristics: on the one hand, the person who is vain is entirely subservient to the estimation of others. His own conscience falls silent before the voice of the crowd. The judgement of God is ruled out. He is far away, invisible, unobtrusive, whereas the crowd is clamorous and arrogant, demanding submission and conformity. Thus subjection to public opinion sets conscience and the judgement of God at naught. On the other hand, a most humiliating thing about it is that the people upon whose opinions we hang are not even those whom we respect. The mob whose applause we crave, the mob of which we are afraid, whose judgement we fear, is not the assembly of saints of God. It is not even made up of people capable of pronouncing a fair judgement, of assessing true values. They are people whose opinions, when they speak of others, we often despise, and yet we fear their verdict. Think of all the things we do in life while keeping an eye on the gallery and wondering whether we shall be well or badly thought of. Were we to pause for a moment we should see that the very people to whom we look for an opinion in our favour or against us, are people whom we consider to have little discernment. And yet we quail before their scrutiny. We court approval on so superficial a plane, in so petty a fashion. In all walks of life we see ourselves and others going the rounds with hands held out, hoping for some wretched coin, a smile or glance of approbation. I have just described the people to whom we turn for alms; but what are the alms and how do we purchase them? By accepting to live in a grotesque world of make-believe, which transforms reality into illusion.

Vanity does not only empty of its real content what we possess. It robs us also of what we actually have. There is a story from the lives of the Desert Fathers of a certain monk who lived in a large monastery and having, as his biographer said, 'contended mightily and having been helped by God, made himself master of nine virtues'. In his endeavour to attain an even greater perfection, he longed however to acquire a tenth one; but despite all his efforts he could not do so. Instead of testing the reasons why he had to strive for more and asking himself whether there was in him any flaw which prevented him from making further progress, he decided to leave his monastery which seemed unfit to foster his striving. As he walked out of his cell, never to return to it, the little humility he had acquired fell off him and vanity spread wider across his soul. He visited in turn nine monasteries, but left them all, one after another, as unqualified to help him to become a saint of God, but every time he left one, he was poorer than when he entered it. He lost whatever patience he had in the first, fortitude in the second, discipline in the third, obedience in the fourth, for-bearance in the fifth, kindness in the sixth, and so forth; but vanity grew stronger and stronger, pride spread wider and wider and brought in its train irritability and anger, slackness, self-will, arrogance, hard-heartedness—and by the time he had visited nine monasteries nothing was left of his original nine virtues that had been first adulterated by vanity and pride and then displaced by their opposites.

There is in vanity another power of destruction: vanity attaches itself to deceptive evidence and to lying appearances. Christ's judgement searches the hearts of men—brushing aside at times the most convincing material evidence, always probing beyond appearances. Two examples may help us realise this: When Christ met Peter on the banks of Tiberias after his Resurrection, he did not charge him with betrayal and claim from him a full confession. He asked him a penetrating question: 'Do you love me more than these?' Had Peter been attentive to what he said, he would have been challenged by the last three words 'more than these'; he might have remembered that Christ had said: 'There was a certain creditor which had two debtors; the one owed five hundred pence and the other fifty. And when they had nothing to pay, he frankly forgave them both. Tell me, therefore, which of them will love him most' and he himself had answered 'I suppose that he, to whom he forgave most'. Had he thought, he might like the prodigal son have come to his senses, but impulsive, rash, sincere as he was, acting before he had given himself time to think, he answers from his heart; 'You know that I love you'. '*Do* you love me?' says Christ again. 'Yes, I do.' 'Do you?' And then Peter suddenly understands! He has already heard this threefold questioning on the night when Christ was betrayed, in the court of the High Priest's palace; he was challenged three times and three times he denied Christ. At that moment Christ's words 'more than these' sound ominous—who will ever believe that he loves him—they spell condemnation not hope. And, desperate, aware that all the evidence is against him, hoping against hope, he says: 'You know all things, you know that I love you.' And Christ—God Who knows indeed the heart of man—knows that Peter does love him. He brushes aside all evidence and speaks to the 'secret man of the heart': 'Follow me.'

Similarly, Christ trusts the woman taken in adultery; he does not break the law but across the evidence, he sees the woman. The adulteress she had been deserved stoning, the woman she has become can enter into Eternal Life. She is no longer the criminal caught in the act; she knows now what she had never known or understood, that sin is the same thing as death. If only she be allowed to live, she will never forget this dread truth, that sin kills. The woman who had committed adultery has died out in her—the one who is waiting in horror to be stoned is another. This one Christ lets go, free, risen, into newness of life. He has seen her heart, has spoken to her deepest self—evidence itself is transcended by a greater truth, not by pity.

As I have said before, there are only two ways of losing our sense of dependence, of subservience to the opinion of others: pride or humility. There is that form of humility which consists in accepting neither men's censure nor their praise, but in remaining simply before the judgement of God and one's own conscience, as in the story of a brother who wanted to know how he should respond to praise and to criticism. 'Go to the graveyard', said his spiritual father, 'and abuse the dead.' He did so and when he came back his father asked him what the dead had done. 'Nothing', said the young monk, 'they remained silent.' 'Go back and praise them,' said the elder. And when his disciple had reported that the cemetery stayed as silent as before, he said: 'Do the same as the dead; human judgement no longer affects them for they stand always in the sight of God.'

There is also that form of humility which is the fruit of labour lost in the service of vanity. It is exemplified in the conclusion to the tale of the monk with the nine virtues. Having lost all he possessed, he arrived at a certain monastery, dejected in spirit and wept because of what had happened to him. He passed judgement on his soul and determined to place his trust solely in the Lord. Having made a full confession to God, he wrote down all the sins of vanity and pride that had brought him so low and placed the piece of paper in his girdle. He came to live in the monastery and whenever temptation befell him, he took out the paper and, reading it, was strengthened against the devil. The brothers were amazed at his tranquillity; neither quarrels among them, nor excitement or perturbation disturbed his serenity. Then they discovered that whenever he was assailed by outward or inward temptations, he drew out from his girdle a paper and immediately peace and strength came to him. 'He is a sorcerer,' they said, 'and his sorceries are in his girdle.' They complained to the abbot to expel him from the monastery, but the abbot thought he would find out about this paper. So in the dead of night he took the paper while the monk was sleeping and read it. And in the morning he said to the brothers, 'I shall read you this paper.' And the monk, afraid that the brothers would see a virtue in his awarenenss of his sins, pleaded with the abbot to keep silent. But the abbot knew that the brothers would learn much from him and commanded the paper to be read. And when they heard what he had written, the brothers fell on their faces saying: 'Forgive us, brother, for we have sinned against thee.'

If we listen to the voice of those around us, we must do so in order to hear the voice of God. Humility is one of the strongest virtues of the Gospel, but we have succeeded in turning it into the feeble virtue of a slave. There are very few people who would like to be humble, because humility seems to be a denial of human dignity. It is the same with obedience: we commend a child for being obedient when he is submissive, when he has no will of his own; we very rarely wonder what is going on in his heart and we too easily mistake the bleating sheep for the sheep of Christ's flock. To be called humble, obedient, meek, is almost an insult. We no longer see the grandeur and the strength of such an attitude.

The caricature of humility which we experience or exemplify ourselves consists in saying hypocritically, when we are praised, that it really is not true; and when we are ignored we draw attention to ourselves by insisting that we are of no account. True humility is born of the vision we have of God's holiness but all too often we try to force ourselves to feel humbler by making ourselves artificially small. I remember an ikon in a church in Moscow with the Lord on his throne, life-size, and, prostrate at his feet, two tiny human figures the size of mice. If you have had a 'pious' Christian education you see only the difference in proportion between God and man, but if you have not learned the language, if you come from outside and simply look at the ikon, you will say: 'No, I want none of that, I am a man, not a mouse. I have no intention of crawling at the feet of this God installed in an armchair. I want to stand upright before him, I do not feel small and I feel free.' If you have read the Scriptures you realise that it is you who are right because it is precisely Christ, God, who gave man the vision of his grandeur and who vindicates his dignity by being the Son of man. When we want to know what man is, we have to look at Christ, the Christ of the Gospels, the Christ of the Mount of Olives, Christ on the cross, Christ resurrected and Son of Man seated at the right hand of the Glory of the Father. We have no need to try to make God greater by making ourselves small and contemptible. God forbids us to do so. And when we do, it is not humility that we attain but an abasement which hinders us from living worthily of the Kingdom of God and of our human calling. How can we at one and the same time grovel at God's feet and become sharers in the divine nature? How can we cringe before this image of God and say: 'I am a living member of this body of which God himself in Christ is the Head? How can we cower at the feet of God and know that we are the Temple of the Holy Spirit, the place of his presence? Can we regard ourselves as petty and of small account before God and yet say, with St Irenaeus, that in the only-begotten Son, by the Holy Spirit, we are called to be THE ONLY-BEGOTTEN SON, the 'totus Christus' and that the glory of God is man fully realised?

Humility, therefore, does not consist in forever trying to abase ourselves and renounce the dignity which God gives us and demands of us because we are his children not his slaves. Humility as we see it in the saints is not born solely of their awareness of sin, because even a sinner can bring to God a broken and contrite heart and a word of forgiveness is enough to blot out all evil from the past and the present. The humility of the saints comes from the vision of the glory, the majesty, the beauty of God. It is not even a sense of contrast that gives birth to their humility, but the consciousness that God is so holy, such a revelation of perfect beauty, of love so striking that the only thing they can do in his presence is to prostrate themselves before him in an act of worship, joy and wonder. When the great experience of the overwhelming love that God has for us came to St Teresa, she was struck to her knees, weeping in joy and wonder; when she arose she was a new person, one in whom the realisation of God's love left her 'with a sense of unpayable debt'. This is humility—not humiliation.

Do we not experience a profound feeling of humility when someone loves us—as always, quite undeservedly? We know that love can in no wise be earned, bought, forced, obtained—we receive it like a gift, like a miracle; there is the beginning of humility. 'God loves us for nothing', says St Tikhon of Zadonsky.

Humility is a way in which one stands before the face of God who sees and man who is unaware of it; it seeks quite naturally the lowest place as water runs spontaneously to the deepest level. It is being entirely open to God, surrendered, ready to receive from him, either from his own hand or through the mediation of other men, never proclaiming one's humble state, for it is not abasement but simply remaining before God in wonder, joy and gratitude.

This is the only means we have of releasing ourselves from the fear of public opinion, from the subservience which frustrates our finding the courage and the opportunity to reform our lives, since we have chosen human values as our criterion. As soon as we have freed ourselves from that we are left with our conscience alone, wherein the voice of God sounds freely, declaring to us the judgement of God and enabling us to begin to live fully and in freedom. We know that we can do this because there are moments when we all break free from public opinion—moments of deep experience that make us full human beings, of true human stature, and our littleness peels off and falls away. When we are seized by great happiness, when sorrow pierces our heart, when we are completely overcome by some inner experience, we are oblivious, if only for an instant, of what other people think of us. When we learn of the death of someone who is dearer to us than all others, we are sunk in grief; we do not ask ourselves if others look upon us favourably or not. When we meet someone we love after a long absence, we do not hesitate to throw ourselves into our friend's arms without wondering whether the crowd will think we are making fools of ourselves.

All this proved possible for Zacchaeus because, brushing aside all human considerations, he was determined to *see* and his determination enabled him to go straight to God, to experience the discovery of the Living God. It is the God of Zacchaeus, the Living God, that every human soul from millenium to millenium is in search of—a God so different from the static images offered by the manifold, successive religions. St Gregory of Nazianzus, in the fourth century, said that when we have gathered from the Scriptures, from tradition and from the experience of the Church, all that man has been able to know of God, and have constructed a coherent image from it, however beautiful the image may be, we have only constructed an idol. Because, as soon as we make an image of God and say: 'Look, this is God', we transform the dynamic, living, unfathomable, infinitely profound God who is our

God, into something limited, of human dimensions, since all revealed knowledge must be of human dimensions, there is nothing in revelation which is not, for if it were otherwise either the infinitely great or the infinitely small would escape us. All that we know of God is yesterday—it is not today or tomorrow. I mean by that that all the knowledge of God that I have at this precise moment, I cannot put before my eyes in order to adore, it is the past, it is the boundary between what was and what will be. The God before whom I place myself in adoration and prayer is the One, the knowledge of whom has brought me to the point where I can meet him beyond human images and rational concepts. I stand before the Unknown God, whose mystery unfolds itself eternally before us yet who remains everlastingly unsearchable.

It is not by inventing new models of God that we shall be able to make people see him. When we persist in saying: 'Centuries ago it was discovered what God is and I am going to tell you' people are not wrong in replying: 'If you knew it would be obvious.' And it is not obvious! If one of us were really a revelation of Christ, we could say: 'I have seen the face of Christ.' You remember the passage in the first Epistle to the Corinthians where St Paul says: 'We have seen the splendour of the glory of God on the countenance of Christ.' There is a similar passage in one of our Orthodox fathers: 'No one can renounce the world unless he has seen the light of eternity at least on the face of a man.' If we were a revelation of this kind, we should have no need to describe God in a thousand ways. In the stories of the Desert Fathers there is an encounter between one of the great masters of the desert and three monks. Two of them ask him endless questions, the other remains silent. At last the father turns to him and says, 'Aren't you going to ask me anything?' 'No', he replies, 'it is enough for me to look at you.' There is another story of a bishop of Alexandria who was coming to visit a monastery. The monks invited one of the brethren to make a speech of welcome but he refused. 'Why?' they asked. 'If he does not understand my silence he will not understand a thing I have to say to him.'

This is the way in which Zacchaeus discovered Christ and in which the Lord spoke to him, as he had silently spoken to Peter on the night of his trial: 'And the Lord turned and looked upon him . . . and Peter went out and wept bitterly.' The God whose gaze searches the deep, 'Who shall not judge after the sight of his eyes' (Isaiah 11.3), 'the Lord who searches the heart and tries the reins' (Jeremiah 17.10), who opens our eyes, sets us free from our pharisaisms and our delusions, and delivers us from our enslavement to the fear of others!

The Parable of the Prodigal Son

A certain man had two sons, and the younger of them said to his father, 'Father, give me the portion of goods that falleth to me.' And he divided unto them his living. And not many days after the younger son gathered all together, and took his journey into a far country, and there wasted his substance with riotous living. And when he had spent all, there arose a mighty famine in that land; and he began to be in want. And he went and joined himself to a citizen of that country; and he sent him into his fields to feed swine. And he would fain have filled his belly with the husks that the swine did eat: and no man gave unto him. And when he came to himself, he said. 'How many hired servants of my father's have bread enough and to spare, and I perish with hunger! I will arise and go to my father, and will say unto him, 'Father, I have sinned against heaven, and before thee, and am no more worthy to be called thy son: make me as one of thy hired servants.' And he arose and came to his father. But when he was yet a great way off, his father saw him, and had compassion, and ran, and fell on his neck, and kissed him. And the son said unto him, 'Father, I have sinned against heaven, and in thy sight, and am no more worthy to be called thy son.' But the father said to his servants, 'Bring forth the first robe, and put it on him; and put a ring on his hand, and shoes on his feet: and bring hither the fatted calf, and kill it; and let us eat and be merry; for this my son was dead, and is alive again; he was lost, and is found.' And they began to be merry. Now his elder son was in the field; and as he came and drew nigh to the house, he heard music and dancing. And he called one of the servants, and asked what these things meant. And he said unto him, 'Thy brother is come; and thy father hath killed the fatted calf, because he hath received him safe and sound.' And he was angry and would not go in: therefore came his father out, and entreated him. And he answering said to his father, 'Lo, these many years do I serve thee, neither transgressed I at any time thy commandment: and yet thou never gavest me a kid, that I might make merry with my friends: but as soon as this thy son was come, which hath devoured thy living with harlots, thou hast killed for him the fatted calf.' And he said unto him, 'Son, thou art ever with me, and all that I have is thine. It was meet that we should make merry, and be glad; for this thy brother was dead, and is alive again; and was lost, and is found.'

Luke 15.11–32

THIS parable is extremely rich in meaning. It lies at the core of Christian spirituality and of our life in Christ; it catches man at the very moment when he turns away from God, forsaking him to follow his own path into this land of dereliction where he expects to find fulfilment and life in abundance. This parable describes also the progress—slow at first and finally triumphant—which brings him back, broken-hearted and freely surrendered, to his father's house.

A first point is that this parable is not simply the story of a single sin. It is sin in its most essential nature which is revealed to us, together with its destructive power. A man had two sons: the younger one claims from his father straight away his share of the inheritance. We are so accustomed to the restraint with which the Gospel depicts the scene that we read it undisturbed—for us it is just the beginning of the story. And yet, if we pause a moment to see what the words really imply, we shall be struck with horror. This simple phrase 'Father, give me . . . ' means 'Father, give me, here and now, what will be mine anyhow when you are dead. I want to live my life, you stand in the way; I can't wait for you to die, I'll be too old then to enjoy what wealth and freedom can bring me: so, be dead! you don't exist for me anymore, I'm grown-up, I need no father, what I want is freedom and all the fruit of your life and labours, die and let me go!' Is not this the very essence of sin? Do we not also speak to God as smoothly as the younger son in the Gospel, but with the same naive cruelty, claiming from God all he can give us, health, bodily strength, inspiration, intellectual brilliance, all that we can be and all that we can have, to take it away from him and squander it, leaving him utterly forgotten and forsaken? Do we not also, time and again, commit this spiritual murder both against God and against our fellow man—children and parents, husbands and wives, friends and relations, companions at school and work? Do we not behave as though God and man were there for no other purpose than to toil and give us the fruits of their lives, their very lives indeed, while they themselves have no ultimate significance for us? People, God himself, are no longer persons, but circumstances or things. And, having taken all they can

75

give, we turn our back on them and find ourselves infinitely far from those who have no face any more for us, no eyes which we can meet. Having blotted out of existence the giver, we become possessors in our own right and exclude ourselves from the mystery of love, because we can no longer receive and we are incapable of giving. This is the very essence of sin—to rule out love, claiming from him who loves and gives that he should go out of our life, accept annihilation and die; this metaphysical murder of love is *the* act of sin, the sin of Satan, of Adam and of Cain.

Once in possession of all the wealth that the 'death' of his father bestowed upon him, without even looking back as young people so lightly-minded do, the young man leaves the dull security of his home and, with a quick step, hastens towards the land where nothing will prevent him from being free: free of constraint, of all moral ties, he can now surrender himself unreservedly to all the impulses of his wayward heart. The past is no more, only the present exists, alluring in its promise, resplendent like a new dawn, and the future lies spread before him, limitless. He is surrounded with friends, he is the centre of everything, life is dazzling and he does not yet suspect that it will not keep its promises. He imagines that it is to him that his new friends cling; the truth is that he is being treated as he treated his father—he exists for his friends only to the extent to which he is rich, only in so far as they can share the glamour of his spendthrift living. They eat, they drink, they make merry; he is full of joy, but how different this joy is from the quiet and deep felicity of the Kingdom of God revealed at the marriage-feast of Cana in Galilee.

But then comes the time when wealth betrays him, and when all is gone and nothing remains to his friends but he himself. According to the inexorable law of the secular and of the spiritual world (Matthew 7.2: 'with what measure ye mete, it shall be measured to you again') they all abandon him, for they never had any use for his person and his fate mirrors that of his father: he no longer exists for them, he is alone and destitute. He is hungry, thirsty, cold, desolate and rejected. He is left alone as he left his father alone but to face an infinitely greater misery—his inward nothingness; while his father, although deserted, was rich with an invincible charity, that charity which made him lay down his life for his son, accept repudiation, so that his son might freely go his way. He finds work, but this is for him greater misery and degradation: no-one gives him any food and he does not know how to find it. And what a humiliation to tend the swine! a symbol of impurity to the Jews, as impure as the demons which Christ cast out. His work is a parable of his state, his interior impurity matches the ritual impurity of his herd of pigs. He has reached rock-bottom and it is now out of the deep that he laments his misery.

We, too, bewail our own misery more often than we give thanks for the joys of our lives, not because our trials are so heavy but because we face them so cravenly, so impatiently. Abandoned by all his friends, rejected on all sides, he remains face to face with himself and for the first time looks inward. Freed from every enticement and attraction, from all the lies and snares which he thought were liberation and fulfilment, he remembers his childhood, the time when he had a father, when he was not an orphan, had not yet become a vagrant without hearth or home. He realises too that the moral murder he committted did not kill his father but him, that his father gave his life with such total love that he can permit himself to hope, and he rises up, leaving behind his precarious existence, sets out for his father's house resolved to throw himself at the feet of his father's mercy. It is not only the memory of his home, of the fire in the hearth and of a table laden with food that makes him start; the first word of his confession is not 'forgive' but 'Father'. He remembers that his father's love was given him freely, and that all the good things of life flowed from it. (Christ said 'Seek ye first the Kingdom of God and all the rest will be added unto you'). He is not going back to a stranger who will not recognise him, to whom he will have to say 'Don't you remember me? There was a time when you had a son who betrayed and abandoned you, it is I'. No, it is the name of 'father' which wells up from the deep, which quickens his pace, which allows him to hope. And in this he discovers the true nature of repentance, for true repentance blends together the vision of one's own evil and the certainty that there is forgiveness even for us because true love can neither falter nor be quenched. When there is only a hopeless vision of our own faults, repentance remains unfulfilled; it brings remorse and may lead to despair. Judas did understand what he had done, saw that his betrayal was irremediable; Christ was condemned, he had died. But he did not remember what the Lord had revealed of himself and of his heavenly Father, he did not understand that God would not betray him as he had betrayed his God. He loses all hope, and goes out and hangs himself. His thought was with his sin, with himself, not with his God, the Father of Jesus and his Father, too.

The prodigal son goes home because the memory of his father gives him courage to return, and his confession springs up, manly and perfect: 'Father, I have sinned against heaven, and in thy sight, and am no more worthy to be called thy son: make me as one of thy hired servants.' He stands condemned before his own conscience, he cannot grant pardon to himself, but there is in forgiveness a mystery of humility which we must learn time and again; we must learn to accept forgiveness through an act of faith in the love of the other, in the victory of love and of life, humbly to receive the free gift of forgiveness when it is offered. And because the prodigal son has opened his heart to his father, he is ready for forgiveness. As he approaches his home, the father sees him, hastens to meet him, falls on his neck, kisses him. How often had he stood on the threshold, looking at the road his son had travelled away from him! He had hoped and waited. And he had now reached the day when his hope was fulfilled. He sees his son who had departed, richly garbed, adorned with jewels, without even a backward glance at the home of his childhood because he had thought and feeling only for the fascinating unknown before him; and this time the father sees him returning a beggar, in rags, utterly dejected, burdened with a past of which he is ashamed and with no future . . . how will his father meet him? 'Father, I have sinned . . . .' But the father does not allow him to disclaim his sonship, as though he were saying to him: 'In coming home you have given me back my life; when you tried to kill me, it was yourself you killed, and now that I am again alive for you, you have come back to life yourself!' And turning to his servants, the father calls: 'Bring forth the first robe and put it on him; and put a ring on his hand, and shoes on his feet.'

Many translations read 'the best robe' but the Greek text speaks of the 'first robe'. Of course, the 'first robe' could be the finest in the house, but is it not more probable that the father said to the servants: 'Go and find the robe my son was wearing on the day he left, the one he dropped on the floor when he put on the garments of treachery'? If they bring him the finest robe in the house, the poor child will feel awkward and dressed up; he will have the impression that he is not at home, but a guest being received with all possible deference and hospitality. One does not wear the best robe in the house when one is comfortably at home. It seems more likely, in the context, to think that the father sends for the robe that the son rejected but the father picked up, folded and put carefully away, as Isaac kept Joseph's coat that his brothers brought back to their father—the coat of many colours, spattered with the blood of the son who must have perished. So now the young man sheds his rags and puts on again the familiar garment, a little worn, the right size, shaped to his body. He is at home in it and looks about him: the years away from his father's house, spent in fornication, perfidy and faithlessness, seem like a nightmare—something that never happened. He is here and he has always been here, wearing the clothes he has always worn. His father is here, a little older, with deeper wrinkles. The servants are here, respectful, watching him with happy eyes. 'He is back with us and we thought he was gone forever; he has returned to life, and we were afraid that in dealing a death-blow to his father he had murdered his eternal soul, destroyed his own life!'

It is a return which blotted out the abyss which cut him off from his father's house. The father goes further —he gives him his ring, which was not just an ordinary ring. You know that in olden times when people did not know how to write, it was the ring with the seal that guaranteed any document. To give one's ring to somebody meant that one was putting one's life, possessions, family, honour—everything—into his hands. Think of Daniel in Babylon, Joseph in Egypt: it was by the giving of a ring that the king committed to them authority to rule in his name. Think of the exchange of rings between two betrothed, an exchange which means: 'I have faith in you, I put myself entirely into your hands. Everything I have, everything I am, belongs to you without reserve.' Do you remember the passage from Kierkegaard: 'When we say "My country, my fiancée", it means not that I possess them but that I belong to them without reserve'?

This parable affords another example of this gift of oneself. The son who had demanded half his father's goods, who wanted to take possession of what he would have after his father's death—the father now puts his trust in him. Why? Simply because he has come home. He does not call him to account for what he did when he was away. He does not say, 'When you have told me the whole story, I shall see if I can trust you'. He does not say as we continually do, explicitly or implicitly, when someone with whom we have quarrelled comes back to us—'Well, I'll take you back on trial; we'll make an effort to patch up our friendship and if I find you faithless, your whole past will rise up again and I shall throw you out because of the past which testifies against you, giving evidence that you will always be faithless'. The father asks nothing. He does not say, 'We shall see'. By implication he says: 'You have come back. The terrible period of your absence— we will wipe it out altogether. Look, the clothes you are wearing show that nothing has happened. You are the same today as you were before you went away. This ring that I am giving you proves that I have no doubts about you. Everything belongs to you because you are my son.' And he puts shoes on his feet that they might be shod 'with the preparation of the gospel of peace', as St Paul writes in the Epistle to the Ephesians.

And the fatted calf is killed for the feast which is the feast of the resurrection—already the feast of life eternal, the banquet of the Lamb, of the Kingdom. The son who was dead is alive; he who was lost in an alien land, a desert land without form and void, as we read at the beginning of the Book of Genesis, has come home. Now the son is in the Kingdom because this Kingdom is the Kingdom of love, of the Father who loves him, of the Father who rescues, reintegrates, restores life.

Now the other son appears on the scene, the son who has always been a good worker in his father's house, and leads a blameless life but who has never realised that the crucial factor in a father-son relationship is not work but the heart, not duty but love. He has been faithful in all things but he has never had a father or been a son except outwardly. Nor has he had a brother. Listen to what he says to his father. Hearing music and dancing he calls a servant and asks what these things mean. And the servant replies, 'Thy brother is come and thy father hath killed the fatted calf, because he hath received him safe and sound'. And the elder son is angry and refuses to go in. His father comes out to entreat him, but he answers: 'Lo, these many years do I serve thee' (and the word *serve* both in Greek and Latin is a strong word, indicating slavery, servitude, having to do all sorts of uncongenial tasks) 'and neither transgressed I at any time thy commandment' (he thinks only in terms of orders and transgressions; he has never grasped the intention behind the spoken words, the heart in the tone of voice, the sharing in the warmth of a common life in which he has his part to play and his father his: it has always been for him a matter of orders and duties which he has never violated). 'And yet', he continues, 'thou never gavest me a kid that I might make merry with my friends: but as soon as thy son was come, which hath devoured thy living with harlots, thou hast killed for him the fatted calf.' Note that he says 'thy son' and not 'my brother': he wants nothing to do with this brother. I knew a family like that—a father and mother, a daughter who was her father's pet and a son who was his affliction; he always said to his wife, 'my daughter' or 'your son'.

We have the situation: 'thy son'. If it were 'my brother' he would not have been like that—he would not have transgressed his father's orders—nor would he have had any fatted calf either. How does the father reply? 'Son, thou art ever with me and all that I have is thine.' The father considers him as a son. For him, he is his son, they are always together. For the son, no: they are side by side—and that is not the same thing. There is no life in common for them, there is no separation—they have the home in common—but neither is there any unity or depth. 'All that I have is thine': the words Christ used in his prayer to the Father before the betrayal. 'And', he goes on, 'it was meet that we should make merry and be glad: for this thy brother was dead and is alive again; and was lost, and is found.'

So the journey is from the depths of sin back to the father's house. That is what lies before us when we make up our minds to live no longer by public opinion but to let the judgement of God be our criterion, heard in the voice of our conscience, revealed in the Scriptures, made manifest in the person of him who is the Truth, the Way and the Life. As soon as we agree to let God and our conscience be our sole judge, the scales fall from our eyes; we are able to see and we know what sin is—an action which denies both to God and to those about us their reality as persons, degrading them into objects who exist only in so far as we can use and abuse them. When we have realised that, we can return into ourselves, release ourselves from the clutches of all that holds us prisoner—return into ourselves and find ourselves face to face with all the blessings of what, for that young man, was his childhood, the time when he still lived in his father's house.

Do you remember the passage at the end of St Matthew's Gospel where Christ told his disciples to go back to Galilee? They had just lived through the most terrible, devastating days of their lives. They had seen their Lord ringed round with hatred, seen him betrayed, they had betrayed him themselves in their weakness. They had succumbed to sleep in the Garden of Olives, and fled when Judas appeared. Two of them had followed from afar their Lord and their God from the house of Caiaphas where they went and sat with the servants, not with him as his disciples. One of them, Peter, who had said during the Last Supper that even if everyone else betrayed him, he would remain true, denied him three times. They had seen the Passion of Christ. They had watched him die. And now they have seen him alive and with them. Judea meant for them the wilderness, devastation, the end of all life and hope. Christ sends them back to Galilee: 'Go back there, where you first knew me, there where we discovered each other in the intimacy of everyday life, where there was yet no hurt, no suffering, no betrayal. Return to the time when all was innocent with infinite possibilities. Go back into the past, deep into the past. Go and teach all nations, baptising in the name of the Father and of the Son and of the Holy Spirit, teaching them all that I have taught you.'

This return within the self leads to the depth where we discovered life, knew life, where we were alive in God with other men. It is from the heart of this oasis in the past, distant or near, that we can start on our road, the road back, with the word 'Father'—not 'Judge'—on our lips, with a confession of sin and hope that nothing has been able to destroy, and with the certainty that God will never accept any degradation of ours, that he will be the guarantor of our human dignity. He will never allow us to become slaves since we are called by the Creative Word and our ultimate vocation to be the sons and daughters of his adoption. We can go to him confidently, knowing that he was waiting for us all the time that we had forgotten him. It is he who will come to meet us as we hesitantly approach the house. It is he who will clasp us in his arms and weep over our wretchedness; a wretchedness we cannot measure because we do not know whence we fell nor how high the vocation that we scorned. We can go to him knowing that he will clothe us again in our first raiment, in the glory that Adam lost in

Paradise. He will clothe us in Christ who is more 'primeval' than the spring freshness in which we were born. He is man as God willed him. It is he whom we must put on, it is the glory of the Spirit that is to protect us when sin would strip us bare. We know now that God, immediately we return to him, will restore his trust in us, give us the ring which empowered Adam to destroy the harmony which God had created and willed, the ring of the only-begotten Son who died on the cross because of man's betrayal and whose death was victory over death and whose resurrection and ascension—our return—are already eschatologically realised in the fullness of the union with the Father.

When we return to this house of the Father's, when we find ourselves face to face with the judgement of our conscience and of God, the judgement is not based on the depth of our theological vision. It is not founded on what God alone can give us in the way of communion with his life. The judgement of God is founded on one thing: 'Are you a human being or are you outside the dignity of man?' In this connection, perhaps you remember the parable of the sheep and the goats in Matthew 25.31–46. 'Lord, when saw we thee an hungred, or thirsty, a stranger, or naked, or sick, or in prison?' If we do not know how to behave as human beings, we shall have no idea how to behave on the divine scale. When we have returned to the Father's house, when we must put on Christ, when the splendour of the Spirit is to take possession of us, when we desire to fulfil our vocation and become true children of the Father, his sons and daughters, we must first and foremost do our utmost to achieve what lies within our power—be human; since fellowship, compassion, mercy are within our capacity, whether we are good or bad.

We can return to the Father. We can return with confidence since it is he who is the seal of our dignity. It is he who wants to save us. It is he who asks of us but one thing. 'My son, give me your heart; all the rest I will add unto you', as it says in Ecclesiasticus. This is the road which leads us all from where we are, blind and outside the Kingdom which we crave to see fulfilled within ourselves and encompassing all things, step by step until we find ourselves before the judgement of God. We see how simple this judgement is, how great should be the hope in us, and how, in this hope, we can make our way to God, confidently, knowing that he is the judge but, above all, the propitiation for our sins, the One to whom man is so dear, so precious, that all life, all death, all the agony and the loss of God, all the hell suffered by the only-begotten Son, is the measure of the value he attaches to our salvation.

The Parables of the Judgement

> Now learn a parable of the figtree; when his branch
> is yet tender, and putteth forth leaves, ye know that
> summer is nigh: so likewise ye, when ye shall see all
> these things, know that it is near, even at the doors.
> But of that day and hour knoweth no man, no, not
> the angels of heaven, but my Father only. Watch
> therefore for ye know not what hour your Lord doth
> come.
>
> *Matthew 24.32,33,36,42*

A THING that has struck me more than once, while I
was reading and preaching certain passages of the
Gospel, is that we proclaim judgement as Good News.
'When you will hear of wars and of rumours of wars,
see that you be not troubled' (Matthew 24.6), 'lift up
your heads, for your deliverance is nigh' (Luke 21.28).
Even the last words of the Book of Revelation: 'Come
quickly, lord Jesus', which were written in hope and
with such longing by the early Church, sound ominous
to many: they would meet them readily with an early
prayer of St Augustine: 'O God, grant it . . . but not
just yet.' To most Christians the very thought of the
judgement of God spells terror; they think of the
possible doom, not of the coming victory of right
(Matthew 12.20) and of God. Very few would make
their own this prayer spoken once by a young man: 'I

love you Lord; if your victory means my destruction, let me perish, but may your victory come!' We forget all too easily the promise of Christ: 'Those who hear my word and believe in it, have eternal life; they do not come to judgement, but have gone from death into life.' These words do not give us a sense of victory because we are not wholehearted enough either in our longing for the triumph of God—whatever the cost to us—or in our faith: even the well-known words 'I believe Lord, help thou my unbelief' are beyond many of us at times.

And yet the judgement *is* good news. It holds a promise that the Lord will come and gather his children and that there will be no suffering and no evil left. But it is good news also in another, more unexpected way: it is obvious from the Bible that we shall not be judged according to any human standards; the yardstick by which we shall be measured is God's absolute and unrelenting claim that love alone counts, and moreover, a love pure of stain and fully expressed in life (James 2). Often this claim seems to be too heavy for us to bear: 'Lord, who can be saved', exclaims Peter. 'This is impossible for man but everything is possible for God', replies the Lord (Matthew 19.25). The very scale—superhuman as it is—of God's claims witnesses to the fact that our vocation is to be the like of God and that nothing smaller than this is worthy of man. In a surprising way this is brought out in the story related by Matthew (22.15–22) of the tribute to Caesar: 'Is it lawful to pay tribute to him or not?' This seems to be a question about citizenship and the social responsibility of the followers of Christ. But it is much more that this, as one of our contemporary divines explains it: 'Why tempt ye me? Shew me the tribute money', answers Christ, and then: 'Whose is the image and superscription?' 'Caesar's.' 'Render therefore, give back, unto Caesar what is Caesar's and unto God what is God's.' What bears the image of Caesar is his own, what bears God's own image, belongs to him: Give to each what is his—the money to him who coined it and impressed it with his sign, but your whole self to him whose image is imprinted in you; we are God's as completely as the tribute money is Caesar's.

We must enlarge our vision a great deal to take in all the range of Christ's parables of the judgement. They do not deal so much with doing as with *being*. At the heart of judgement there is faith: does not the Lord himself say: 'He who believes shall be saved'? but a faith far, far greater than anything to which we are accustomed: 'These signs shall follow them that believe; in my name shall they cast out devils; they shall speak with new tongues; they shall take up serpents; and if they drink any deadly thing, it shall not hurt them; they shall lay hands on the sick, and they shall recover' (Mark 16.17–18).

But if this be strictly, formally true, who can stand before the judgement of God? No one, indeed, if justice is to be meted out according to human rules of retribution, but 'we have an advocate with the Father, even our Lord Jesus Christ and He is the propitiation for our sins'; he who says 'I have not come into the world to judge the world but to save it' (John 9.39). Before whom are we then to stand? Who will condemn us? Two witnesses will stand against us on the Day of the Lord—our conscience and Word of God. The Gospels say: 'Agree with thine adversary quickly, whiles thou art in the way with him; lest at any time the adversary deliver thee to the judge, and the judge deliver thee to the officer, and thou be cast into prison. Verily I say unto thee, thou shalt by no means come out thence, till thou hast paid the uttermost farthing.' Spiritual writers have often identified this adversary as our conscience, the natural and God-given knowledge of right and wrong, of which Paul speaks in his Epistle to the Romans: 'When the Gentiles, who have no know-ledge of the law, act in accordance with it by the light of nature, they show that they have a law in them-selves; their own consciences endorse the existence of such a law for there is something which condemns or commends their actions. We may be sure that all this will be taken into account in the day of true judgement, when God will judge men's secret lives by Jesus Christ.' Another accuser will be God's own word, 'it is not I that judge you but the word which I have spoken', that word which is truth and life, to which all our being responds, which can quicken us and yet which we so carelessly discard. 'Were not our hearts burning within us, while he talked with us by the way?' say the pilgrims returning from Emmaus. And yet, so often, Christ must sadly observe: 'I have come a light into the world, but men have preferred darkness because their deeds were dark.'

The Parable of the Talents (Matthew 25.14–30). The Lord gives everyone of his servants a 'talent according to his several abilities'. He makes them as rich of possibilities as they can sustain and will never ask from them anything more than he has himself given. Then he leaves us free, not abandoned, not forgotten, but unhampered, free to be our true selves, free to act accordingly. However, a time of reckoning will come, a summing-up of all our life. What have we done with all that was possible? Have we become all we could, borne all the fruits we might have borne? And why have we fallen short of God's faith in us and frustrated his hopes? To these questions several parables give an answer. In the one we are discussing we see that instead of trading with his talents, that is, putting them to use, and in so doing, risking them, the unfaithful servant 'wrapped his only talent (his life, his being, himself) in a napkin, digged the earth and hid his lord's money'. Why did he do that? First of all, because he was timid and cowardly—he was afraid of risk. He could not face the fear of a loss and of its consequence, responsibility. And yet, to risk nothing is to gain nothing. In our own lives cowardice does not apply solely to the material goods we sit on, like a hen on her eggs and, unlike her, without ever hatching out anything! It applies to everything in our lives, indeed to our life itself. To be sure to go through life unscathed we hide in an ivory tower, close our minds, stifle our imagination, harden our heart, make ourselves as insensitive as we can, because, above all, we are afraid of being hurt, wounded—and we become at best like those little marine organisms that, frail and vulnerable, secrete a hard shell which will keep them safe, but also imprisons them in an unyielding coral armour which slowly kills them. Security and death are co-relative. Only risk and insecurity are compatible with life.

So, it is cowardice which is the unfaithful servant's and our first enemy. But—does not Christ advise us to be wise and not undertake more than we can achieve in two of his parables? (Luke 14.28–32). What is the difference between the unworthy servant and ourselves on the one hand, and the wise, thoughtful men he wishes us to be? It lies in two things. The men described by Christ were willing, ready, eager to risk. They had a daring spirit of enterprise. It was not stifled or smothered by prudent considerations; they only measured their strength against the odds and acted with realism, which is also a form of obedience and humility. Their spirits soared high; they were prepared to be among those 'who take the Kingdom by violence', 'who lay down their lives' for their friends or their God. The servant whom his master cast out was unwilling to take any risk; he preferred never to enjoy what he had been given rather than endanger himself by losing it.

And here we face another aspect of the parable: why was he (why are we) so frightened? Because we see God and life as he saw his master: 'I knew that thou art an austere, a hard man, reaping where thou hast not sown, gathering where thou hast not scattered, and I was afraid and I hid my talent and lo, there thou hast that is thine.' He slanders his master as we slander God and life. 'I knew thou art hard, what is the point of trying?' 'Have thy own!' But what is it which is God's own? The answer can be found, as I have said, in the parable of the tribute money. His own is our all! When we give it back or if he takes it back—nothing is left either to us or of us. Both these thoughts are expressed in the Gospel: 'Take away from him the talent and cast the unprofitable servant into outer darkness; from him that hath not shall be taken away even that which he hath.' That is, his very being, his reality itself, or as Luke puts it 'even what he imagines he possesses', that is, the talent which he has hidden away, left unused, taken away both from God and man. In a most tragic way Christ's words come true: 'By thy words shalt thou be justified and by thy words shalt thou be condemned.' Did not the servant, do we not, say: 'I knew you for a hard master'? But then, is there no hope? Indeed there is! And it rests on the Lord's warning which is also a promise: 'By what judgement you judge, ye shall be judged also' and 'judge not that ye be not judged', which St Paul underlines in the following way: 'Who art thou, that judgest another man's servant? To his master he standeth or falleth.' All these passages are clearly illustrated in another of Christ's parables, that of the wicked servant in Matthew 18.23–35: 'O thou wicked servant, I forgave thee all that debt, because thou desiredst me: shouldest not thou also have had compassion on thy fellow servant, even as I had pity on thee? So likewise shall my heavenly father do also unto you, if ye from your hearts forgive not every one his brother their trespasses.'

Yet it is not only because we are cowards and malign both God and life that we are unfit to stand before the judgement of God. The 24th and 25th chapters of the Gospel according to St Matthew, together with its parallels, give us more clues.

The Parable of the time of Noah (Matthew 24.37–41) *and the Parable of Lot* (Luke 17.28–30). What was wrong with these men? They were good-humoured, cheerful, easygoing people. They did nothing wrong. Why did the flood come and engulf them? Is it not because, on the one hand, they did no right (yet life does not consist in abstaining from doing wrong, that is, from 'scattering', but in doing right, that is in 'gathering' with Christ our God, Matthew 12.30) and, on the other hand, because they had become 'flesh', that is, lost all spiritual quality, become good, tame, and greedy brutes? How much does this apply to us? We are so prone to let go of spiritual endeavour, of constructive but costly effort, of selfless struggle, to be easygoing, and weak and to say: 'I'm doing ho harm! Even if I sin privately, what does it do to others? I am kind, pleasant, easy to live with. Whom does it concern that I enjoy my pleasures, smoke and drink immoderately, gamble and . . . ?' Alas, it does! And that because we are no disposable pieces of a material whole but live members of each other, so that in us and because of us, the whole of mankind is being robbed of the Spirit of God, of a potential saint of God!

A second way in which we come under sentence is shown in the *Parable of the Evil Servant* (Matthew 24. 45–51). This man is not even good-humoured and kind. He wants pleasure. He sees that the Lord is slow to come (Is he really slow? Is Peter not right when he says: 'God is not slack, he is long-suffering'—11 Peter 3.9) and he takes advantage of his master's absence, of the power and scope it gives him to gratify his desires at the other servants' expense. Beware! he is not so different from the good-humoured contemporaries of Noah and of Lot, or from us; only he is greedier, circumstances give him power to satisfy his appetites, his viciousness and his craving for domination. He also enjoys impunity, for a while, and delights in it. He knows he is doing wrong, he relishes evil, he probably laughs at his absent master. How easy it is for man to slip from kindness into ferocious brutality; how quickly pussy can become what she always is at heart—a beast of prey! Watch then! Does not the Lord himself warn us: 'Sin lieth at thy door' (Genesis 4.7), 'watch therefore: for ye know not what hour your Lord doth come; therefore be ye ready, for in such an hour as ye think not, the Son of man cometh' (Matthew 24.42–44).

And again a new warning reaches us through the *Parable of the Ten Virgins, of the Ten Bridesmaids* (Matthew 25.11–13).

Shall I be frank? I do not like the wise virgins. I would have preferred them to give all their oil to the foolish ones, to be cast out for their sakes (Romans 9.1–3), in a generous act of folly; but this was not the point Christ was making. His point was—'Watch'! How much of us sleep our life through? We call it day-dreaming or being imaginative. But in all truth it is slumber; reality becomes a dream, while dreams acquire cogency and our days themselves become nights and our lives sleep-walking. Besides is it not enough to close one's eyes for it to be night, for us to be entitled to sleep? Are we not all benighted! And does God not speak to our condition in the words of Isaiah (51.17): 'Sleepers arise!'? Are our lights still aglow? Are we wise bridesmaids? Are those of us who find the wise virgins selfish, less selfish than they? Are we capable of awaking from our dreams, cheerful and loving, willing to sacrifice the little reality that is ours (a last glow in our sinking lamps) for others who have also been awakened by a cry in the night, but discover with horror that no reality whatsoever has survived their dreaming? Sleep, dream, unreality—is that all there is in us? Shall the Day of the Lord come upon us like a thief to rob us of all, all, all? Shall it be darkness and terror and wailing for us?

Where can we find ground for hope? Paradoxically —unexpectedly enough—in the *Parable of the Sheep and the Goats* (Matthew 25.31–46).

For some unaccountable reason this parable is quoted more than any other as an image of the judgement, a statement about its hopeless finality. Yet it tells us something essential, not about dying and doom or salvation, but about living: neither the sinners nor the just are asked anything by God about their convictions or their ritual observances; all the Lord appraises is the degree to which they have been human: 'I was thirsty, and ye gave me drink: I was a stranger, and ye took me in: naked, and ye clothed me; I was sick, and ye visited me: I was in prison, and ye came unto me.' Being human requires, however, imagination, a sense of humour and of occasion, and a realistic and loving concern for the true needs and wishes of the object—or shall we say the victim—of our care. Here is a story from the lives of the Desert Fathers to illustrate this point. After a full, brilliant social and political life at the court of Byzantium, St Arsenius retired into the desert of Egypt, seeking for complete solitude and contemplative silence. A lady of the court, who had been a great admirer of his, sought him out in the wilderness. She fell at his feet. 'Father', she exclaimed, 'I have undertaken this perilous journey to see you and hear from you just one commandment which I vow to keep all my life!' 'If you truly pledge yourself never to disobey my will, here is my commandment: If you ever hear that I am in one place, go to another!' Is not this what many would say to all those do-gooders whose virtue they are doomed to endure?

To me, the point of the parable of the sheep and the goats, is this: if you have been truly and wisely human, you are ready to enter into the divine realm, to share what is God's own, as Eternal Life is nothing else than God's own life shared by him with his creatures. 'Having been faithful in little things, we shall be given great ones'; having been worthy of the earth, we shall be capable of living the life of Heaven, partaking of the nature of God, filled with his Spirit. If we be good stewards in what was not our own (all the gifts of God) we shall come into what is our own, as is so powerfully shown in the parable of the unjust steward (Luke 16.1–12).

This long meditation on some of the parables of the Judgement should urge us to go inward and search our own life and our own soul, and here is a pattern for such self examination which I offer as a mere, but useful, suggestion. It is taken from *The Way of the Pilgrim*,[1] a Russian spiritual classic of the nineteenth century.

'Turning my eyes carefully upon myself and watching the course of my inward state, I have verified by experience that I do not love God, that I have no love for my neighbours, that I have no religious belief, and that I am filled with pride and sensuality.

1. *I do not love God*: For if I loved God I should be continually thinking about him with heartfelt joy. Every thought of God would give me gladness and delight. On the contrary, I much more often and much more eagerly think about earthly things, and thinking about God is labour and dryness. If I loved God, then talking with him in prayer would be my nourishment and delight and would draw me to unbroken communion with him. But, on the contrary, I not only find no delight in prayer, but even find it an effort. I struggle with reluctance, I am enfeebled by sloth, and am ready to occupy myself eagerly with any unimportant trifle, if only it shortens prayer and keeps me from it. My time slips away unnoticed in futile occupations, but when I am occupied with God, when I put myself into his presence, every hour seems like a year. If one person loves another, he thinks of him

1 Translated by R. M. French, SPCK (1954).

throughout the day without ceasing, he pictures him to himself, he cares for him, and in all circumstances his beloved friend is never out of his thoughts. But I, throughout the day, scarcely set aside a single hour in which to sink deep down into meditation upon God, to inflame my heart with love of him, while I eagerly give up twenty-three hours as fervent offerings to the idols of my passions. I am forward in talk about frivolous matters and things which degrade the spirit; that gives me pleasure. But in the consideration of God I am dry, bored and lazy. Even if I am unwillingly drawn by others into spiritual conversation, I try to shift the subject quickly to one which pleases my desires. I am tirelessly curious about novelties, about civic affairs and political events; I eagerly seek the satisfaction of my love of knowledge in science and art, and in ways of getting things I want to possess. But the study of the Law of God, the knowledge of God and of religion, make little impression on me, and satisfy no hunger of my soul. I regard these things not only as non-essential, but in a casual way as a sort of side-issue with which I should perhaps occupy my spare time, at odd moments. To put it shortly if love for God is recognised by the keeping of his command- ments (if ye love Me, keep My commandments, says our Lord Jesus Christ), and I not only do not keep them, but even make little attempt to do so, then in absolute truth the conclusion follows that I do not love God. That is what Basil the Great says: "The proof that a man does not love God and His Christ lies in the fact that he does not keep His commandments."

2. *I do not love my neighbour either*: For not only am I unable to make up my mind to lay down my life for his sake (according to the Gospel), but I do not even sacrifice my happiness, well-being and peace for the good of my neighbour. If I did love him as myself, as the Gospel bids, his misfortunes would distress me also, his happiness would bring delight to me. But, on the contrary, I listen quite undisturbed to curious unhappy stories about my neighbour or, what is still worse, I find a sort of pleasure in them. Bad conduct on the part of my brother I do not cover up with love but proclaim abroad with censure. His well-being, honour and happiness do not delight me as my own, and, as if they were something quite alien to me, give me no feeling of gladness. What is more, they subtly arouse in me feelings of envy or contempt.

3. *I have no religious belief*: Neither in immortality nor in the Gospel. If I were firmly persuaded and believed without doubt that beyond the grave lies Eternal Life, I should be continually thinking of this. The very idea of immortality would terrify me and I should lead this life as a foreigner who gets ready to enter his native land. On the contrary, I do not even think about eternity, and I regard the end of this earthly life as the limit of my existence. The secret thought nestles within me: Who knows what happens at death? If I say I believe in immortality, then I am speaking about my mind only, and my heart is far removed from a firm conviction about it. This is openly witnessed to by my conduct and my constant care to satisfy the life of the senses. Were the Holy

Gospel taken into my heart in faith, as the Word of God, I should be continually occupied with it, I should study it, find delight in it and with deep devotion fix my attention on it. Wisdom, mercy, love, are hidden in it; it would lead me to happiness, I should find gladness in the study of the Law of God day and night. In it I should find nourishment like my daily bread and my heart would be drawn to the keeping of its laws. Nothing on earth would be strong enough to turn me away from it. On the contrary, if now and again I read or hear the Word of God, yet even so it is only from necessity or from a general love of knowledge, and approaching it without any very close attention, I find it dull and uninteresting. I usually come to the end of the reading without any profit, only too ready to change over to secular reading in which I take more pleasure and find new and interesting subjects.

4. *I am full of pride and sensual self-love*: All my actions confirm this. Seeing something good in myself, I want to bring it into view, or to pride myself upon it before other people or inwardly to admire myself for it. Although I display an outward humility, yet I ascribe it all to my own strength and regard myself as superior to others, or at least no worse than they. If I notice a fault in myself, I try to excuse it; I cover it up by saying, "I am made like that " or "I am not to blame". I get angry with those who do not treat me with respect and consider them unable to appreciate the value of people. I brag about my gifts; my failures in any undertaking I regard as a personal insult. I murmur, and I find pleasure in the unhappiness of my enemies.

If I strive after anything good it is for the purpose of winning praise, or spiritual self-indulgence or earthly consolation. In a word, I continually make an idol of myself and render it uninterrupted service, seeking in all things the pleasure of the senses, and nourishment for my sensual passions and lusts.

Going over all this I see myself as proud, adulterous, unbelieving, without love to God and hating my neighbour. What state could be more sinful? The condition of the spirits of darkness is better than mine. They, although they do not love God, hate men, and live upon pride, yet at least believe and tremble. But I? Can there be a doom more terrible than that which faces me, and what sentence of punishment will be more severe than that upon the careless and foolish life that I recognise in myself?'

Judgement would hold nothing but terror for us if we had no sure hope of forgiveness. And the gift of forgiveness itself is implicit in God's and people's love. Yet it is not enough to be granted forgiveness, we must be prepared to receive it, to accept it.

All too often forgiveness is offered, but we recoil from it: to our pride forgiveness sounds like an ultimate humiliation, and we try to eschew it by putting on false humility: 'I cannot forgive myself for what I have done, how could I accept to be forgiven. I appreciate your goodness, but my conscience is too exacting, too sensitive for me to take advantage of your kindness', and it is words like 'kindness' we would use, to make the gift which is proffered as insignificant as possible and our refusal as frustrating as we possibly can for our generous friend. Of course, we cannot, we should never forgive ourselves! It would be monstrous if we could; it would simply mean that we take very, very lightly the blow which we have dealt, the wound which we have inflicted, the pain, the misery, the hurt which we have caused. (And, alas! we do this whenever we are impatient at the sight of someone whom we have hurt and who seems to be pained 'beyond measure'. 'How long are you going to sulk? oh, stop crying! Have I not already said to you that I am sorry; what else do you want?' Such phrases mean, if translated into plain speech: 'I have forgiven myself long ago; how much more am I going to wait for you to forgive me?'). God forbid that we should ever be able to forgive ourselves, but we must learn both never to allow this to happen and also to accept, to receive the free gift of another's pardon. To refuse to do so is tantamount to saying, 'I do not really believe that love blots out all sins, neither do I trust in your love.' We must consent to be forgiven by an act of daring faith and generous hope, welcome the gift humbly, as a miracle which love alone, love human and love divine, can work, and forever be grateful for its gratuity, its restoring, healing, reintegrating power.

One should not expect to be forgiven because one has changed for the better; neither should one make such change a condition for forgiving other people; it is only because one is forgiven, one is loved, that one can begin to change, not the other way round. And this we should never forget, although we always do.

Also we must never confuse forgiving with forgetting, or imagine that these two things go together. Not only do they not belong together, but they are mutually exclusive. To wipe out the past has little to do with constructive, imaginative, fruitful forgiveness; the only thing that must go, be erased from the past, is its venom; the bitterness, the resentment, the estrangement; but not the memory.

True forgiveness begins at the moment when the victim of injustice, of cruelty, of slander accepts the offender as he is, for no other reason than the fact that he has come back, like the Prodigal Son whose father asked no questions, made no claims, set no conditions for his reintegration into the household. God's forgiveness is ours from the moment when God takes upon himself the burden and all the consequences of our fall, when the Son of God becomes the Man of Sorrows (Isaiah 52–53). It is emphatically not when we become a Saint! God has already granted forgiveness when he has said: 'I am ready to die for you: I love you.' This is also where forgiveness begins between human persons. If in a family crisis the offender simply comes back, too proud or too shy, or perhaps too cramped by fear, to say much, his redemption begins at the very moment when his family say to him: 'But we never ceased to love you; let go of your fear; we still love you—oh, the pain of it! now that you are back we shall all be healed.' And this, the person who is *right* can do and should do, because it is so much easier for him to do than for the person who is in the wrong; also because those who are right share with the offenders the reponsibility of the rift, of the quarrel and must atone for it also. Theirs must be the first steps towards reconciliation. I remember a man of some standing who once came to see me and told me that a friend of his who claimed no small spiritual achievements had offended him: 'Who should go and make his peace with the other?' he asked. 'I cannot answer your question', I replied, 'as I cannot possibly set myself as a judge between you, but one thing is certain to me: the meanest of the two of you will wait for the other to make the move.' The great man said no word, but went forthwith to make his peace with his friend. Vanity had done what neither humility, nor wisdom, nor even simple friendship had been able to achieve. How sad . . . How different was the generous, loving, free forgiveness which the Father granted his Prodigal Son!

Yet, in neither case was forgiveness the end of all problems: in the faraway, strange country of dereliction, the rejected offender cannot but have learnt ways which are repellent to his family and friends: the smell of the swine may well still cling to the body of the Prodigal Son, and the habits of his wayward life will not vanish overnight; he will have to unlearn them gradually, possibly very slowly; he may, he is bound to have lost many of the more refined manners of his original surroundings; he will have to learn them again, slowly. And the family will be able to reintegrate, to regenerate and redeem him only to the extent to which its members will remember (not forget) his weaknesses, the flaws in his character, the bad habits acquired by him. But remember without resentment, without a feeling of superiority, without a feeling of shame, but with the pain of compassion, with that compassion which makes 'grace abound where sin is present'; with the will and a stern determination never to forget what there is that the beloved one should be shielded from—his natural frailty, his acquired weakness. Otherwise he who needs our healing and protecting help will be submitted to overwhelming temptation and become the victim of never-ending, bitter recrimination. To forgive and to put under probation are two very different things. To forgive means to accept the other 'as Christ has received us', to 'bear one another's burden' as he bears ours, simultaneously those of the victim and of the offender, loving joyfully, gratefully, the ones, loving the others sacrificially, with the joy of self-offering.

This is God's way. His Cross witnesses to his faith in mankind and in every single man, his unconquerable hope; this is why his death becomes our life, and his Resurrection—Eternity itself for us.

THE GOAL

The Resurrection and the Cross

For the Jews require a sign, and the Greeks seek after wisdom: but we preach Christ crucified, unto the Jews a stumblingblock, and unto the Greeks foolishness; but unto them which are called, both Jews and Greeks, Christ the power of God and the wisdom of God. Because the foolishness of God is wiser than men; and the weakness of God is stronger than men.

1 Corinthians 1.22–5

O Death, where is thy sting?
O Hell, where is thy victory?
Christ is risen and the demons
                    have fallen.
Christ is risen and the angels
                    rejoice.
Christ is risen and life exults.
Christ is risen and there is none
dead in the tomb. For Christ is
raised from the dead, and
become the first-fruits of them
that slept. To Him be glory and
dominion from all ages to all
ages. Amen.

St John Chrysostom

WE must at no moment forget that the end of our journey is our meeting with the Risen Christ. Some people, whilst admitting the importance of the Resurrection in the experience of the Apostles, wonder how this apostolic experience can have the same central significance for us; but is it enough for us simply to believe in the words of others and to found our faith on something totally unverifiable? I would like to stress the fact that, of all the historic events in the world, the Resurrection of the Lord belongs equally to past history and to present reality. Christ, dead on the Cross on one particular day, Christ, risen from the tomb in his glorified, human flesh on one particular day, belongs to the past as an historic fact; but Christ, once risen, living forever in the glory of the Father, belongs to the history of each day and each instant, because living, according to his promise, he is with us, now and always. Christian experience from this point of view is essentially attached to the event of the Resurrection, because it is the one event in the Gospels which can become part of our own personal experience. All the rest we receive from tradition, written or spoken —the account of the Crucifixion, the different events told us by Holy Scripture—but the Resurrection, this we know personally, or else we are ignorant of the primordial, essential fact of the Church's life and the Christian faith. St Symeon the New Theologian said: 'How can one who knows nothing of the Resurrection in this life, expect to discover and enjoy it in his death?' Only the experience of the Resurrection and Eternal Life can make the death of the body into sleep and death itself into the Gate of Life.

If such a plain, peremptory statement arouses questions, demands a response, demands of you that you ask yourselves whether you are within Christian experience, so much the better! Here is the central

of the Apostles than the death of a
and a leader. They did more than mo
beloved friend, the defeat of a leader t
would triumph. If we read the G
from the point of view of the rela
between the Apostles and the Lord,
by little, an identification grows bet
and his disciples. Having come to hir
of faith, others sceptically; 'Can any
out of Nazareth?' (John 1.46), havir
all the vicissitudes of hesitation ar
being completely won not only by wh
but by his whole personality, we see
Crucifixion, forming a group whi
described as separated from the v
sense of 'chosen and redeemed'. (
their absolute centre of life. Wher
his disciples and asked them if th
leave him, Peter replied: 'Lord, to
Thou hast the words of eternal lif
human group, centred round some
Life made manifest in a transitor
the world into which human sin i
corruption; and this human grou
from this relation to Christ, not b
by affection, friendship, loyalty,
they have already the experience
new dimension, a dimension not
ontological, substantial. It is no
fuller, richer, more beautiful; it is
Christ has brought them.

experience without which
there is no Christianity, with
faith but credulity; not 'th
seen' but the capacity to ac
an unverifiable witness, a v
nothing more than that son
which seems incredible
for reasons equally incredi
accept.

Let us now turn to this ev
ask ourselves why it is so c
say, 'If Christ was not rais
most miserable, for our faith
was not raised, our whole fa
inner life, our hope, all is
founded on something wh
which cannot serve as the f

Let us now think, separa
twelve Apostles. St Paul, as
Hebrews, pupil of the gr
burning faith, grounded in
faithful to the tradition of
could have met Christ, St
contact with Christ's discipl
undone in order to know,
this new prophet—compari
all he had understood in He
ness of the Hebraic commu
Christ. With all that he
Messiah, he had not been a
when he came. It was with

And when Christ died on the Cross, rejected, betrayed by those who stayed outside this circle of love, this mystery of divine, present, incarnate, active, transfiguring love, it is not just a question of the death of a friend and master; it is a far greater tragedy. If it were possible for Christ, with all that he represented, to die upon the Cross, this meant that human hatred was stronger than Divine Love; human hatred had managed to repulse Divine Love, to banish him from the habitations of man, had rejected him and killed him on Calvary. And this death of Divine Love, this rejection, is accompanied by the loss, also, of the presence of Eternal Life in the midst of mankind: it has been cast out. Divine Love, which had been offered to man in such a way as to be both a reproach and a great hope, this Divine Love is rejected, and without it, what remains to man? Just that which was always theirs, twilight in which to struggle, separated from Christ, a twilight consisting of a little affection, a little hatred and plenty of indifference, a twilight in which men are strangers to one another, where relations are fragile, held together by ties which break repeatedly, by attachments which disengage and dissolve.

But what of those men who were united to Christ, who had experienced the presence of the Living God in their midst? All that remained was the possibility of enduring, of continuing to exist, but no more to live. Since they had tasted Eternal Life, the ephemeral life of time which ends in corruption and death was no more than a prospect of the final defeat, a postponement of the return to dust—that which could no longer be called life but was a 'pre-death'. So that when Scripture by means of images or direct words, makes us understand that in the death of Christ we are all dead, to the degree that we are profoundly identified and allied to him, and that in his Resurrection we come back to life with him, Scripture is speaking to us of something very precise and real. But there is here something which we cannot grasp with the same tragic darkness as that which filled the Apostles, and for a very simple and obvious reason, namely, that on Good Friday, whatever effort of imagination we make to dwell only on the tragedy, we know precisely, that before the end of three days we shall be singing of the Resurrection. We cannot obliterate our knowledge of Christ's Resurrection: not only because year after year we have experienced it and we cannot artificially forget it, but because as members of the Body of Christ, as Christians integrated into the mystery of Christ—the total Christ which is the Church—we have within us this Eternal Life which witnesses to the fact that the darkness of Good Friday is already overcome; within us it is already overcome, within us the light is already present, life is already present, victory, partially at least, is already won. And for us it is impossible not to remember the coming Resurrection although we are in the midst of Good Friday.

But for the Apostles, Good Friday was the last day of the week and the last day of life as they had known it; on the following day, the day which preceded the Resurrection, the darkness was as dense, as obscure, as impenetrable as it had been on Good Friday, and if the Resurrection had not happened, all the days of the year and all the days of their life would have been days of total darkness, days when God was dead, when God had been conquered, when God had been definitely and radically exiled from the community of men. And if you bear in mind the unity which was gradually created between Christ and his disciples, so that the life they lived was his life, in him and through him they moved, saw, perceived and understood, you will grasp that his death was not only this total and irremediable darkness of Good Friday—for them the last day of history—but it was also their own death because Life had been taken away from them; they could no longer live but merely exist.

Thus you will understand why, for the Apostles, the Resurrection was such a complete renewal, such a decisive event: when Christ, on the third day, appeared to them, all the doors being shut, their first thought was that it was an hallucination, an apparition. And Christ on that occasion, as on all the occasions of his appearance after the Resurrection related in the Gospel, insisted on the fact that he was not a ghost, not an illusion, but a true corporeal presence. He shares food with them. And we also understand why Christ's first words are words of peace. 'Peace be unto you!' He brings them the peace which had been taken from them by his death, which was their death; he released them from the utter, hopeless confusion in which they were submerged, this twilight state wherein Life was unrecognisable, this transitory life from whence Eternity had been driven; and he gave them that peace which he had promised, that peace which only he could give, that 'peace which passeth all understanding', the peace of reintegration into Life, beyond all doubt, beyond all hesitation—the certainty possessed by men who, because they are alive, cannot doubt Life, the life of the world to come, already come, by means of Christ's Resurrection and the gift of the Holy Spirit.

The joy of the Resurrection is something which we, too, must learn to experience, but we can experience it only if we first learn the tragedy of the Cross. To rise again we must die. Die to our hampering selfishness, die to our fears, die to everything which makes the world so narrow, so cold, so poor, so cruel. Die so that our souls may live, may rejoice, may discover the spring of life. If we do this then the Resurrection of Christ will have come down to us also. But without the death on the Cross there is no Resurrection, the Resurrection which is joy, the joy of life recovered, the joy of the life that no-one can take away from us anymore! The joy of a life which is superabundant, which, like a stream runs down the hills, carrying with it heaven itself reflected in its sparkling waters. The Resurrection of Christ is reality in history as his death on the Cross was real, and it is because it belongs to history that we believe in it. It is not only with our hearts but with the totality of our experience that we know the risen Christ. We can know him day after day as the Apostles knew him. Not the Christ of the flesh, not Christ as he was seen in bewilderment by people who surrounded him in the days of his earthly life, but the everliving Christ. The Christ of the spirit of whom St Paul speaks, the risen Christ who belongs to time and eternity because he died once upon the Cross but lives forever. The Resurrection of Christ is the one, the only event that belongs both to the past and to the present. To the past because it did happen, on a given day, in a given place, at a given moment, because it was seen and known as an event in time, in the life of those who had known him. But it belongs also to every day because Christ, once risen, is ever alive, and each of us can know him personally, and unless we know him personally we have not yet learnt what it means to be a Christian.

Let us go back to Good Friday, the day when Christ died upon the Cross that we may live. A Russian hymn says:

O Life Eternal, how is it that Thou art brought to the grave,
O Light how is it that Thou art quenched?

Indeed it is Life Eternal that seems to go down to the grave. It is Light Eternal, the glory of God revealed to us in his Son that seems to be quenched, to be removed from us forever. To understand the meaning of Good Friday, of the saving death of Christ, we must understand the meaning of the Incarnation. Each of us is born into time out of non-being. We enter a fleeting, precarious life in order to grow into the stability of Eternal Life. Called out of naught by the creative word of God, we enter into time but within time we can find eternity, because eternity is not a never-ending stream of time. Eternity is not something—it is Someone. Eternity is God himself, whom we can meet in the ephemeral flow of time and through this meeting, through the communion which God offers us by grace and love in mutual freedom, we can also enter into eternity to share God's own life, become in the daring words of St Peter 'partakers of the divine nature'.

The birth of the Son of God is unlike ours. He does not enter time out of naught. His birth is not the beginning of life, of an evergrowing life; it is a limitation of the fullness that was his before the world began. He who possessed eternal glory with the Father before all ages, enters into our world, into the created world, wherein man has brought sin, suffering, death. Christ's birth is for him not the beginning of life, it is the beginning of death. He accepts all that is inherent in our condition and the first day of his life on earth is the first day of his ascent to the Cross.

His death has a quality, a weight, which belongs to him alone. We are not saved by the death of Christ because it was particularly cruel. Countless men, women and children throughout the ages have suffered as cruelly. Many have burnt in flames, many have frozen in the ice, many have died of long, excruciatingly painful illness, many have suffered torture and imprisonment in camps in the horrors of war. The death of Christ is unique because Jesus of Nazareth could not die. It is not his Resurrection which is the incredible miracle. It is his death. We know from the writings of St Paul, from the faith indeed of the whole Church, that death is the result of sin, sin being understood as our severance from our communion with God. And Christ is God himself incarnate; united to his Godhead, his very humanity, his true humanity is beyond death, the incarnate Son of God makes his very flesh, his very human nature incorruptible and beyond dying. And yet he dies. Here lies the paradox and here is the tragedy, the tragedy unequalled. One of the saints of the Orthodox Church tells us that in the Incarnation of Christ two events take place. On the one hand, he becomes man, but he reveals to us the real humanity to which we are called—a humanity which is rooted in the divine life itself, inseparable from God, unconquerable by death. But to become one of us, to share with us truly, our suffering and our dereliction, Christ takes upon himself all the crushing weight of the human condition, all the limitations which otherwise are alien to his glorious humanity: the pain and the weariness, hunger and thirst, and the very possibility of death, and when the hour comes, he dies our death upon the cross, but a death which is more than ours. We die because we die out, our body decays and falls away, we can no longer live. If in the course of this transitory life we have acquired the knowledge of God, a common life with him, then dying no longer means for us a defeat but a new abundance and fullness of life, as St Paul sees it when he says that for him to die does not consist in losing life, but of being clad, vested in the life of eternity. But dying is always a tragedy for us; body and soul are parted, the completeness of the human being is broken up and we must wait for the resurrection of the body and the victory of Life Eternal to become truly, fully, what we are called to be.

But in the death of Christ something different happens. He dies although he cannot die, he dies although he is immortal, in his very human nature inseparably united with his Godhead. His soul, without being separated from God, is torn out of his body, while both his soul and his flesh remain united with the Godhead. He will lie in the tomb incorruptible until the third day, because his body cannot be touched by corruption. It is full of the Divine Presence. It is pervaded by it as a sword of iron is pervaded by fire in the furnace, and the soul of Christ descends into hell resplendent with the glory of his Godhead. The death of Christ is a tearing apart of an immortal body from an immortal soul—of a body that could not die from a soul that is alive, remains alive forever. This makes the death of Christ a tragedy beyond our imagining, far beyond any suffering which we can humanly picture or experience. Christ's death is an act of supreme love; he was true when he said, 'No-one takes My life from Me, I give it freely Myself'. No-one could kill him—the Immortal; no-one could quench this Light which is the shining of the splendour of God. He gave his life, he accepted the impossible death to share with us all the tragedy of our human condition.

The Lord himself has thus taken upon his shoulder the first cross, the heaviest, most appalling cross, but after him thousands and thousands of men, women and children have taken upon themselves their own crosses, lesser crosses, but how often these crosses, which are lesser than Christ's, remain so frightening for us. Innumerable crowds of people have lovingly, obediently, walked in the footsteps of Christ, treading the long way, the tragic way which is shown by our Lord, a way tragic but which leads from this earth to the very throne of God, into the Kingdom of God. They walk, carrying their crosses, they walk now for two thousand years, those who believe in Christ. They walk on, following him, crowd after crowd, and on the way we see crosses, innumerable crosses, on which are crucified the disciples of Christ. Crosses, one cross after the other, and however far we look, it is crosses and crosses again. We see the bodies of the martyrs, we see the heroes of the spirit, we see monks and nuns, we see priests and pastors, but many, many more people do we see, ordinary, simple, humble people of God who have willingly taken upon themselves the cross of Christ. There is no end to this procession. They walk throughout the centuries knowing that Christ has foretold us that they will have sorrow on this earth, but that the Kingdom of God is theirs. They walk with the heavy cross, rejected, hated, because of truth, because of the name of Christ. They walk, they walk, these pure victims of God, the old and the young, children and grown-ups. But *where are we*? Are we going to stand and look; to see this long procession, this throng of people with shining eyes, with hope un-quenched, with unfaltering love, with incredible joy in their hearts, pass us by? Shall we not join them, this eternally moving crowd, that is marked as a crowd of victims, but also as little children of the Kingdom? Are we not going to take up our cross and follow Christ? Christ has commanded us to follow him. He has invited us to the banquet of his Kingdom and he is at the head of this procession. Nay, he is together with each of those who walk. Is this a nightmare? How can blood and flesh endure this tragedy, the sight of all these martyrs, new and old? Because Christ is Risen, because we do not see in the Lord who walks ahead of us the defeated prophet of Galilee as he was seen by his tormentors, his persecutors. We know him now in the glory of the Resurrection. We know that every word of his is true. We know that the Kingdom of God is ours if we simply follow him.